RANGERS:

THE LOST DECADE

MARK COOPER

INTRODUCTION

This is a book about the events at Rangers from 2010 to 2020. It was a decade in which Rangers went from playing at Old Trafford to Balmoor, Peterhead. A decade in which Rangers clinched three titles in a row and then went on an unprecedented trophy famine. A decade 'lost' to the club as it sought to recover from the damage wreaked upon it. A decade in which everything that could go wrong, did go wrong. And yet a decade in which, as it ended, the club began to re-emerge as Scotland's premier club once again.

ONE

November 2010 - May 2011

On November 18, 2010, the news broke that Craig Whyte was on the verge of buying Rangers from David Murray in a reported £32m deal. It was a huge story and the initial question was who exactly was Craig Whyte? The media coverage did a lot to influence supporter opinion and expectation of Whyte in the early days. There was talk of Whyte being Scotland's youngest ever self-made millionaire, of millionaire playgrounds in Monaco, of Highland castles and, of course, infamously, a £1 billion fortune. The reality was very different.

Although it was later claimed that Whyte was a mystery figure who had managed to erase his past, his business record was there to be found, at least in part and certainly enough to ring alarm bells. What was clear, for anyone that looked, was that Whyte's business dealings consisted of failed companies, non-payment of taxes, non-payment of creditors, unpaid employees, transfer of company assets, a byzantine company structure and a millionaire lifestyle on the back of it. It was a business history riddled with failure and unpaid debts.

His company, Vital UK Ltd, a group dealing in security and cleaning, went into voluntary liquidation in 1996 owing £750,000. The report from the liquidators suggested that Whyte had transferred the assets of the company to the Bahamas. He had also failed to register some employees for PAYE. Vital UK went under owing £280,000 in income tax, £33,000 in VAT and £66,000 in trade and expenses. Whyte would airily dismiss the collapse of his companies and complain about "people with an axe to grind". His lawyers stated in the High Court that he owed a single creditor £3.5m. Whyte later claimed this was "a tactic" by his legal team and that he didn't owe this amount. Unpaid workers were down to an "administrative error".

Whyte had fled to Monte Carlo in 1999 owing HMRC, creditors and employees. He resurfaced in Scotland in 2008 when it was reported that he had purchased Castle Grant in Grantown-On-Spey. A previous visitor attraction, Whyte claimed to have been in discussions with Historic Scotland over a multi-million pounds restoration of the castle. Historic Scotland said they had no record of any such discussion. A disconnect between what Whyte said and what actually happened would be a recurring theme in his story.

When Whyte's interest in Rangers became public in November 2010, the Scottish media showed very little restraint in their coverage. An avalanche of largely misinformation appeared in the press and not always from the usual sources. Writing in The Times of November 19, 2010, Graham Spiers wrote of how Whyte "knew Rangers inside out" and "had the opportunity to make a real success of Rangers over the coming years". Spiers also lamented the negative coverage given to David Murray in his later years at the club and, presumably without a hint of irony or self-awareness, sneered at "the erstwhile compliant journalists" who were behind some of it.

Robert McAulay in The Sun on the same day attributed a personal wealth of "£1bn" to Whyte which was down to "shrewd investments". The idea that a Scotsman, in the small business world of Scotland, could become a billionaire, even with shrewd investments, and no-one knew who he was or how he did it simply wasn't challenged enough. The Sun even had an insider assuring their readership that Whyte's specialty was "nursing stricken companies back to full health". A comical reading of Whyte's business history.

The Herald did at least acknowledge that Whyte's career had "not been without its knocks", mentioned the collapse of a company in the early 1990's and that another company was on the verge of being struck off by Companies House before launching into a breathless round-up of Whyte's "considerable personal wealth".

In this environment, it's not difficult to see why many in the Rangers support were happy to go along with the takeover. The media coverage of the prospective new owner had been largely positive and optimistic, if not completely wrong. Who wouldn't want a 'billionaire fan' taking over your club?

The collective failure to properly scrutinise Whyte prior to the takeover was disastrous for Rangers. Any seeds of doubt that any supporter may have had were largely shouted down over a larger narrative of a 'venture capitalist' who had gone abroad and made lots of money somehow and was now coming back to Scotland to save Rangers. The Scottish media had, inexplicably, come to be regarded as running a pro-Rangers bias. It was difficult to see how such lazy reporting and regurgitation of PR puff pieces had served Rangers' interests in any way at all.

The biggest surprise about the Whyte move was that he'd made it at all. Rangers were at the beginning of an ongoing dispute with HMRC over payments to Employee Benefit Trusts (EBT's). The matter had been referred to a First Tier Tax Tribunal which had, initially, been due to sit in the autumn of 2010. HMRC had first contacted Rangers about alleged tax due from these Trusts earlier in the year even though the Trusts had been running since 2001. HMRC were reportedly seeking in the region of £36m plus penalties believed to be around £14m. Quite clearly, any buyer of Rangers would protect themselves against taking on such a bill. That would be the sensible thing to do. Indeed, early reporting of Whyte's takeover suggested Murray and Lloyds Bank were amenable to indemnifying Whyte against any adverse outcome in the First Tier Tax Tribunal.

It was also reported that Whyte was in business with Andrew Ellis, who had popped up a year earlier in a bid for the club. The proposed deal was a £30m outlay which would see Whyte own 75% of the club and Ellis the other 25%.

It didn't take long for Whyte's 'billion pounds' persona to start to crumble. Just days after his move on Rangers had went public, he was served a writ for £90,000 by a company called One Stop Roofing which was owned by the then Albion Rovers manager Paul Martin. The company had carried out work for Whyte on his home in Grantown-on-Spey in June 2009 and had yet to be paid. This too would be a regular feature.

Lloyds Bank had been exerting a tight grip on the club for nearly two years and had appointed Donald Muir to the Rangers board to, effectively, get their money back. The Murray Group was also under serious pressure. Lloyds were not Murray's bankers of choice. He'd had a long-standing relationship with the Bank of Scotland. They had supported his business for many years and he was especially good friends with Gavin Masterton. This relationship extended into Scottish football. Masterton was involved at Dunfermline Athletic, the Bank of Scotland had sponsored the SPL from 1999 to 2007 and was the friendly bank to many Scottish football clubs. The 2008 financial crash brought an end to much of this.

The Murray Group had ventured heavily into commercial property which, suddenly, wasn't worth quite as much as it used to be. The Bank of Scotland was also in a perilous condition. It was effectively taken over, under pressure from Prime Minister Gordon Brown, by Lloyds. Lloyds had no interest in Scottish football and certainly had no interest in carrying lots of debt north of the border. The Murray Group owed Lloyds £700m and Lloyds had taken on 18% of the company in February 2010, taking their stake to 30%, in return for a reduction of £150m of debt. The climate suddenly got much colder. The tide had gone out and lots of people had no clothes on.

Yet, thanks in the main to success on the pitch under Walter Smith, Rangers' debts had almost halved from £35m in 2007 to around £18m in 2011. The club owed Lloyds £18m but on a turnover of £50m, this should not have been a huge problem. The gorilla in the room, as chairman Alastair Johnston called it, was the big tax bill. Lloyds did not want them or the Murray Group holding that bomb if or when it went off. It could certainly be argued that Lloyds had a duty to protect themselves and their shareholders from any significant increase in the Murray Group debt. But the Murray Group had initiated the EBT scheme and, indeed, ran it on behalf of Rangers – a service for which Rangers paid them £500,000 a year. Lloyds were also carrying a great deal of Murray Group debt, in any case.

It was against this backdrop that Whyte was making his move. The initial claim was that the takeover would see Whyte (and Ellis) paying around £30m with a guarantee of £25m to be spent on the playing squad over five years – around £5m a year separate from European income or any other revenue. This was no triviality or frivolous spending. Rangers had been unable to sign a player from August 2008 to August 2010, an inconceivable situation for a club of Rangers' size. The bank had been putting on the squeeze and every expenditure had to be approved. Walter Smith and his group of players had worked wonders to continue their success but many, including Smith, were reaching the end of the road. The team needed a refresh and an injection of new talent.

The release of Rangers' interim results in April 2011 threw another spanner in the works. A second tax bill of £2.8m had been uncovered in the due diligence conducted as part of the Whyte bid. It dated back to 2000 and to payments made to Tore Andre Flo and Ronald de Boer. Despite the bill coming from 'left field', the club accepted it and it was not disputed as the big tax bill had been. The First Tier Tribunal which had sat before Christmas 2010 was due to restart again in April 2011 with, it was hoped, a verdict by the summer of 2011.

Chairman Alastair Johnston was part of an informal independent board committee (IBC) which had been set up by the board to scrutinise any bids for the club. They did not have the power to block any takeover but they could delay it and certainly issue warnings about any potential buyer. As well as Johnston, the committee included chief executive Martin Bain, directors John McClelland, Donald McIntyre and John Greig.

Johnston gave an interview in early April where he attempted to highlight the seriousness of the problem. "It is quite likely that the HMRC impact on the club and the Murray group might not be determined to October or November. It is a 10,000lb gorilla wandering around the room, and we don't quite know what its appetite is." Yes, the club's debts had been reduced to under £20m and, yes, the club had a trading profit of £23m over the previous 18 months. But Johnston was pointing to a much bigger problem that needed to be addressed. It was the kind of problem that led Johnston to ask Whyte when he met him – "What are you doing here?" It was not enough to hope that the Murray Group would indemnify the club against any HMRC impact.

The IBC were becoming more and more alarmed. At a meeting in April, they had attempted to present to Whyte and his advisors how to manage the club over the season, the cashflow ups and downs of a football club over a year. They had shown no interest. Whyte's projections of the funds required to run the club, including the potential HMRC liability, were vastly different from the board's own expectations and personal experience.

Johnston was widely criticised for even floating the possibility that Rangers could go into administration as a result of the HMRC dispute. It was scaremongering and irresponsible, said his critics. Many of the same critics would later criticise Johnston, and the board at this time, for not doing more to stop Whyte. Yet beyond public questioning, what could they do? They knew something was 'off' about Whyte's bid but without precise details and evidence, what could be done? And what if there was evidence? Would the bid have still been forced through regardless?

Around the same time, a private investigation into Whyte's background, commissioned by a third party, came into the possession of chief executive Martin Bain. It listed some of Whyte's many achievements, including failed companies, unpaid tax and unpaid creditors. Bain presented the findings to David Murray and pleaded with his boss to block the Whyte bid. Bain had been something of a protégé of Murray's, going from a humble male model in the

1990's, rising through the Murray Group and becoming chief executive of Rangers in 2005. Murray's indebtedness to Lloyds had left him no room to move, he said. He told Bain that he had no option but to sell. He asked Bain to convert the rest of the board to the benefits of the Whyte deal. Bain's refusal to endorse the Whyte bid ended his relationship with Murray.

Johnston and the board desperately sought out an alternative. It arrived in the shape of a £25m bid from Dave King and Paul Murray. This offered to pay Lloyds £15m (of the £18m they were owed), buy out David Murray's shareholding and then provide £10m to Ally McCoist for players. There would then be a share issue, underwritten by King to around £20m, to provide additional funding to the club. Unlike Whyte's offer, though, it did not involve replacing the Lloyds debt with a debt to King. King's offer also foresaw the need to maintain a working credit facility, ideally with Lloyds in the short-term, to manage the football club over a season. Whyte's offer would close off the club's credit facility leaving it entirely reliant on Whyte's own funding. Paul Murray, among others, saw the club running out of cash very quickly under Whyte's offer.

The only downside to King's offer, and it was not a downside from a Rangers point of view, was that any potential HMRC liability would reside with the Murray Group and, thus, with Lloyds. Johnston had couched the objection with the Whyte bid carefully -

"We are still awaiting a detailed working capital statement demonstrating that there is sufficient funding in place to meet the pressing needs of the club." This was putting it mildly.

There was considerable media pressure to downplay and deride the alternative offer from Dave King and Paul Murray and some members of the press were only too happy to play along. "A disruption", "their deal makes no sense", "back of a fag packet job" "Whyte's deal will secure the future of the club". There was even whispers that Lloyds would withdraw the club's overdraft if Whyte's deal did not go through. Johnston would subsequently claim he received such a call from Lloyds on the day that Whyte officially took over.

The unavoidable conclusion is that the Dave King and Paul Murray offer stood no chance as Lloyds would not have entertained any other offer that did not involve the potential HMRC liability being taken on by another party. Whyte's offer involved paying Lloyds and not much else. It left little room for player investment, stadium maintenance, let alone any potential bill from HMRC.

Days before Whyte's deal was concluded, Paul Murray tried once again to warn supporters – "It is vitally important that every fan understands what could be about to happen to our club. The wrong move now could lead us down an even more difficult path. Of course, debts have to be paid. But Craig

Whyte's offer is weighted in favour of the bank rather than the club even though we have a debt level which is more than manageable." In particular, Murray cast serious doubts on Whyte's ability to steer Rangers through any issue with HMRC – "In my opinion Craig Whyte has not adequately demonstrated what his strategy is for managing and funding a negative outcome on this matter."

The pleas of Johnston, Murray and others were to fall on deaf ears. On May 6, 2011 Craig Whyte bought David Murray's shareholding in Rangers for £1. The independent board committee, in one final jab, published a statement on the Rangers website. It read – "Although the IBC has no power to block the transaction, following its enquiries the IBC and Wavetower [Whyte's company] have differing views on the future revenue generation and cash requirements of the club and the IBC is concerned about a lack of clarity on how future cash requirements would be met, particularly any liability arising from the outstanding HMRC case." The statement was pulled from the website later that day.

TWO

May 2011 - February 2012

Whyte's first move was to appoint Phil Betts to the board. Betts had accompanied Whyte down Edmiston Drive prior to the match against Hearts on May 7. Supporters were trying to shake Whyte's hand, pleased that a new era was beginning and the fiscal parsimony of Lloyds appeared to be gone.

Two days before Whyte took over, Celtic had lost 3-2 at Inverness in the league. Rangers were only three wins away from the title. In Walter Smith's last match in charge, Rangers stormed into a 3-0 lead at Rugby Park after just seven minutes. They went on to record a 5-1 win and clinch the 54th league title in the club's history. It had been 20 years since Smith had won his first title and perhaps no manager since Struth had sustained such an influence on the club over such a long period. No-one would know it but it would be the last of such days for a long time to come.

The full Stock Exchange announcement of the takeover had stated that Wavetower had purchased Rangers. Betts and Whyte were both directors of Wavetower which was, in turn, owned by Liberty Capital, which was wholly owned by Craig Whyte. He also began to unveil his strategy for dealing with

HMRC which seemed to consist of bravado and bullishness – "Our advice is that we are going to win the case. I'm confident we are going to win the case and there will be no liability there."

Gary Withey was appointed company secretary. He worked for Collyer Bristow LLP and had advised Whyte during the takeover. On May 23, Alastair Johnston and Paul Murray were removed from the board by Whyte after they had both refused to resign. Chief executive Martin Bain and finance director Donald McIntyre were both suspended pending contractual issues. Dave King would also be asked to resign. Directors John McClelland and John Greig would be allowed to stay.

Johnston had already agreed to step down on May 15 and had only wanted to stay on to oversee a circular to be sent to all shareholders outlining Whyte's financial commitments to the club. This was scheduled to happen on or before June 6. Whyte's desire to remove Johnston early was revealing. Johnston did not leave the scene quietly and issued a warning for supporters to be vigilant regarding Whyte - "I will say - as a lifelong Rangers fan and a real one - that the 26,000 other shareholders in Rangers, as well as the hundreds of thousands of other supporters, need to remain vigilant and continue to exert pressure on Mr Whyte to support the club financially as he has publicly committed to do."

The circular arrived on June 6 and revealed that Wavetower Limited, Whyte's company to front the takeover, had been renamed the Rangers FC Group Limited. The three directors were Whyte, Betts and Andrew Ellis. The £18m debt to Lloyds had certainly been paid although the actual source of the funds was not revealed. The debt now resided with Rangers FC Group Limited and would be waived, said Whyte, with the exception of one circumstance. And that is if the club suffers "an insolvency event within 90 days of an appeal in relation to the tax claim brought against it by HMRC". The circular also promised £5m for investment in the playing squad for 2011/12, £1.7m to fund improvements in the kitchens and the PA system and around £3m for the small tax bill that had been received, and not disputed, by the club earlier in the year. In the case of an insolvency event, however, that £9.7m would be added to the £18m used to pay Lloyds meaning Rangers FC Group Limited would be owed around £28m.

On June 14, the Daily Record's Keith Jackson ran an article about the existence of a document at Companies House called an MG50. The document was in the names of Craig Whyte and Phil Betts and had been filed the previous month. The Daily Record believed that this document pointed to Whyte's intention to mortgage off the next four years of season ticket money as a security against "some form of loan". The detail was lacking but the truth was there. Rumours and suspicion about season ticket money and, of course the source of Whyte's funding, was starting to gather pace. Naturally, the story was rubbished by Whyte and some of the Daily Record's rivals. With a neck of brass, one insider told The Sun that the form was intended to "ring fence the money so it cannot be used as security".

Whyte continued to make crowd-pleasing and crowd-distracting appointments. Former Rangers player and former chief executive of the SFA, Gordon Smith, was recruited as Director of Football whilst former Hearts and Scottish Rugby executive, Ali Russell, was brought in as a commercial and business director. Both appointments were welcome. Many supporters had been calling out for a Director of Football for years to bring some modern thinking to the setup at Ibrox and Smith was a popular, intelligent voice in the game. Many also felt that the club's commercial side could be revamped and made more profitable.

It was all very well, however, bringing people in to do certain jobs. You had to then let them do it. Learning something in the mastery of smoke and mirrors, supporters were also promised other shiny things. A luxury hotel, shopping centre, luxury flats, restaurants, presumably of the luxury kind, were all promised as part of some revamp of the Govan area that Whyte imagined could be tied to the Commonwealth Games.

Whyte was tapping into what supporters wanted to hear. The David Murray era had largely petered out as Murray became less involved in the daily running of the club from around 2002 onwards. Murray had often boasted that he'd never had a night out in Glasgow which, presumably, was meant to indicate he was not caught up in the West of Scotland concerns. On a personal level, this is fine. On a corporate level, it meant Rangers suffered from a disengagement from political and cultural circles. It was not regarded as important. This meant the club was marginalised from public discussions and had become an easy target. Whyte's rhetoric about Rangers' enemies, such as the BBC, and his promise to defend the club in matters such as Scotland's fake debate on sectarianism, was music to some supporters' ears. Desperate for someone to stand up for them and the club, here at last was someone who understood the concerns of the support. It was populism and, for Whyte, it worked, for a short time at least.

In an interview with The Herald on June 20, Whyte continued to insist that the takeover had all been done with his own money and that 'there was no bank debt'. On the same day, Martin Bain sued Rangers for breach of contract. Bain claimed he had read in the newspaper that he was being replaced and, indeed, that he would not be returning to Rangers at all. He resigned as a director but not as chief executive. Rangers responded by claiming Bain had offered to resign in March 2011 and that they were "investigating a number of serious allegations and are seeking his response to a number of legitimate questions we have of him."

At a preliminary hearing in the Court of Session in Edinburgh, Bain's counsel Charles Cowie said his client was "very keen" to progress with the action. Rangers wanted to launch a counterclaim to claim back "excessive monies" they alleged had been drawn by Bain from the club. The case was held over until October by Lord Menzies to allow both parties to make adjustments to their pleadings.

Despite claiming in the circular sent to shareholders in June that almost £3m had been set aside to pay the small tax bill, Whyte decided in August to appeal against it claiming that he'd simply inherited it from the old regime. The fact that the 'old regime' had transparently informed Whyte of the bill, it had been included in the club's accounts, and that he'd agreed to pay it as part of his takeover, and in his circular to shareholders, was seemingly not his responsibility. The matter was to escalate within weeks when sheriff officers arrived at Ibrox to serve legal papers on the club over the matter.

It was suggested that the bone of contention for Whyte was the 'fine' component of the liability. The club was happy to pay the £2.8m, it was said, but not the £1.4m penalty for late payment. This, it was claimed, was all that was being disputed. When sheriff officers returned to Ibrox in early September, a Rangers source said it was simply "more paperwork being delivered". However, in fact, an arrest order had been issued to the club's bank and £2.8m, that Whyte claimed he was happy to pay, was moved into a holding account on the orders of HMRC. It would remain there for 14 weeks pending any objection from Rangers. If there was no objection, the money would go to HMRC.

A Rangers spokeswoman would bleat that "enough is enough, we are sick and tired of HMRC leaking these negotiations." As had happened throughout Whyte's glittering business career, failure to pay, court orders, accounts frozen were all regarded as 'tactics' or 'negotiation'. It was an illusion of control in a sea of absolute chaos.

The problems would continue. Law firm Levy & MacRae, which had carried out work for the club earlier in the year, had been forced to sue the club for around £35,000 after their bills had gone unpaid. There was no mention from Whyte or his spokeswoman whether this was part of a negotiation. More worryingly, when the matter was settled out of court, Jonathan Brown, counsel for Levy & MacRae, informed Lord Hodgson at the Court of Session that there was a "real concern about solvency of the club". This was dismissed by the club as "unfounded".

Back in court in other matters, the Martin Bain case was still rolling on. A 14-page document drawn up by his legal team was leaked online in September. It also questioned the solvency situation of Whyte's Rangers. Unsurprisingly, Bain's team drew attention to the upcoming First Tier Tax Tribunal, now expected in November 2011, and which had around £49m riding on it. It was anticipated that Whyte's Rangers would not be able to pay such an amount in the event of an adverse outcome. The document also claimed that season ticket money had been "assigned for the next four years to a London finance company in exchange for cash flow" by Whyte – a claim denied by him in June.

The bad news and online leaks may have appeared like a whispering campaign but for so much of it actually being true. It was certainly true to say that the club, even before Whyte, had a problem managing information and public perception. None of this had helped the club to breathe and function as a normal business for a long time. Nonetheless, the court appearances of the Whyte era were down to his own erratic management of the club at that time.

Looking to head off the doomsayers, Whyte gave an interview on Rangers' website where, without understatement, he said there had not been a queue of people waiting to buy Rangers. He did not speculate as to why this might have been. The cheery optimism of May had now given way to warnings of "difficult decisions in the next few months". He did not rule out administration in the event of the tax tribunal verdict going against the club and nor could he. Paul Murray, Alastair Johnston and Dave King had said as much six months earlier.

Over the summer, a series of targets wanted by Ally McCoist had eluded the club. Dundee United's David Goodwillie had been regarded as the prime target. Valued at £2m by United, Whyte went public that he did not consider the valuation as realistic. He offered £1m. By the time he came to meet United's valuation, the player was at Blackburn having a medical. Perhaps it was considered safe then to make the offer knowing it didn't need to be followed through. Carlos Cuellar, Craig Conway and Neil Danns were among the players McCoist had wanted but didn't get. Whyte had promised £5m of his own money in player investment. It was time to work down the list of the players McCoist could get.

As HMRC had sought to freeze money, now it was Martin Bain's turn. Bain was suing the club for £960,000 and had wanted to freeze that entire amount lest Rangers lose the HMRC big case and be unable to pay. Lord Hodge at the Court of Session agreed to a figure of £480,000. Whyte was furious and, for once, made not an unreasonable observation – "I find it breathtaking that the former chief executive, who was in post when this issue [the

HMRC big case] emerged, has now sought fit to seek legal protection from its potential consequences." Touche. In the same interview, Whyte continued to obfuscate on the source of his wealth, trying to bamboozle the reader with business jargon – "We do all sorts of deals, public to private, commodity trading, Forex, a wide variety, but we try and keep it low key."

On September 16, Roddy Forsyth wrote that the issues at Rangers under Whyte were somehow related to the arrival of Graeme Souness some 25 years earlier. He even went so far as to say that Rangers had "simply reaped what they once sowed". It was a bizarre theory and yet one which would occasionally pop back up. It would only make sense if Rangers' problems in 2011 were related to Rangers' spending in the Souness years or even the 1990's or that Rangers had a mountain of debt at all. None of that is true. Rangers did not have a debt issue when Craig Whyte took over.

Forsyth referred to "wage inflation" and Souness "pillaging the England international side". It's a strange mindset that thinks reversing the trend of players heading south was a bad thing for Scottish football or that Scottish players had no right to earn more than they did. Indeed, the late 1980's saw every club in the top flight in Scotland record an increase in average attendances as supporters came back to a revitalised game. Forsyth was indulging in a faux nostalgia for a time that never existed. He made a snide reference to the Ibrox redevelopment being "largely funded by Rangers Pools" as if this was money that appeared out of thin air rather than the pockets of Rangers fans. Nor was it clear why clubs being made to bring their stadia into the 21st century was a negative for which Rangers were directly or indirectly responsible. This kind of narrative seemed motivated more by jealousy than fact.

Following in the footsteps of Martin Bain, finance director Donald McIntyre quit the board five months after being suspended but did not quit as an employee. He then took the club to court for £300,000 in damages and, inevitably, sought to have the sum arrested in the club's bank account. This was followed by the resignations of John McClelland and John Greig from the board. All three cited "being excluded from participating in corporate governance at the club" as reasons for their resignations. Since Whyte had arrived, almost the entire board, with the exception of Dave King isolated in South Africa, had gone.

On October 20, 2011, BBC Scotland broadcast a documentary entitled "Rangers: An Inside Story" which revealed previously unknown information about Craig Whyte. The biggest revelation was that Whyte had been banned as a director for seven years from June 2000 in relation to his company, Vital Holdings. There were also allegations from the Insolvency Service of fake auditors, misleading accounts, company funds being taken out to pay tax bills but tax bills not being paid and acting in a company whilst disqualified. Whyte responded with all the bluster and wind that he could manage. He claimed that the programme was a "prejudiced muckraking exercise" and said he would instruct his lawyers, Carter Ruck, to sue the BBC. No writ would ever materialise.

Whyte also withdrew the co-operation of Rangers from the BBC and accused the organisation of running a "negative" campaign against Rangers. This was clear deflection but it was also, in many respects, true. This made it difficult for the programme to be taken seriously amongst large sections of the Rangers support. BBC Scotland had not shown itself to be trustworthy in the past in respect to its coverage of Rangers so why would this be any different? The source was contaminated and BBC Scotland had a credibility problem with the Rangers support. A situation that exists to this day.

The 2011/12 season had begun with a major fall-out between Rangers and the BBC over a national news broadcast on July 22 which appeared to show Ally McCoist smirking at a press conference in response to a serious question about sectarianism. The BBC said it had been an "inappropriate edit" but did not say how it had happened. Yet it was difficult to conceive of circumstances where McCoist would be shown responding to an entirely different question unless the intention was to reflect the

Rangers manager in the worst possible light. It is little wonder that any genuine information that the programme might produce was lost in what seemed to be a propaganda war waged by the BBC.

And yet the programme did contain genuine information. As well as the Whyte revelations, there was also an appearance by ex-chairman Alastair Johnston who had been forced out by Whyte five months earlier. He repeated that Lloyds had leaned heavily on Rangers to accept the Whyte deal and that in the due diligence on Whyte carried out by the IBC they had been unable to establish the personal wealth that Whyte had claimed to possess.

Whyte's response to this latest peeling back of the layers was to come out flailing and swearing. "A lot of f****** nonsense" was his considered response. He claimed the club was in its best shape for years. The club certainly had been doing well prior to Whyte's arrival. The annual results, released in December 2011, showed a near 50% reduction in net debt to £14m in the 12 months to June 30, 2011. The club also reported increased turnover at £57m, increased expenses at £47.5m and a pre-tax profit of £76,000. Whether the club was still in good shape in December 2011 was debatable.

The news of Whyte's previously undisclosed director ban prompted the launch of an SFA investigation in December. The SFA had a "fit and proper person criteria" but, by its own admission, these criteria were "illustrative and not exhaustive" though they did include people who had been disqualified as directors within five years of becoming involved in clubs. Any potential penalties were unknown and no penalties had ever been issued in the past for a breach. It was clear as mud. The SPL didn't have a "fit and proper person criteria" with the concept itself being dismissed by chief executive Neil Doncaster as having "no track record of success."

The release of the accounts also meant that an AGM would have to be called by December 31, six months after the financial year end. The auditors Grant Thornton, however, had not signed off on the accounts due to concerns over long-term financial sustainability in relation to the HMRC tax case. The First Tier Tax Tribunal which was meant to sit in November had now been kicked into January 2012. The delay was unhelpful. The AGM was postponed by Whyte until the first quarter of 2012, ostensibly because "we'll have a better indication of how the tax case will play out."

Both the club and Whyte ended 2011 back in court. The £300,000 compensation claim brought by Donald McIntyre was settled although the settlement was not disclosed. Whyte himself was back in court in his £90,000 personal dispute with One Stop Roofing. Alistair Clark QC, for the company, said Whyte may have an "unreliability problem" or a "credibility problem."

At the end of January, the Daily Record returned to its claim from June that Whyte had mortgaged season ticket money for an unspecified purpose. This time they fleshed out the detail. Whyte had used the money to fund the takeover of Rangers and, in a precursor of things to come, HMRC were also investigating the non-payment of VAT by Whyte at the club since May.

Whyte had borrowed £24.4m from Ticketus and this time he didn't bother denying it. Bizarrely, he stuck to his claim that the £18m debt to Lloyds had been repaid by his own company. The claim his takeover had effectively been funded by the fans own season ticket money was, said Whyte, "categorically untrue". He claimed that many clubs had used Ticketus and that was certainly true. Rangers had used Ticketus in the past for working capital. But not to fund their own buy-out. Ticketus had normally been used by Rangers towards the end of a season. At a club like Rangers, with large numbers of season ticket holders fronting money over the summer, there can be a dip come April or so just before season ticket money is due. The most Rangers had borrowed previously was £5m. Now the Rangers support was paying for Whyte's purchase of the club.

Money was borrowed against season ticket sales for seasons 2011-12, 2012-13 and 2013-14. This had secured £24.4m for Whyte. How you are able to borrow money on an asset (season ticket money) that you didn't currently own would need to be explained much later. On June 27, 2011, Ticketus had requested a payment of £9.5m – their share of the 2011-12 season ticket money – but Whyte was only able to offer £3.5m. He did the only sensible thing that a responsible and credible owner would do in such circumstances and borrowed an additional £6m from Ticketus, to pay Ticketus, and this time mortgaged sales from 2014-15 to fund it. This was using the credit card to pay the credit card.

The IBC had consistently questioned Whyte's source of wealth and how he was going to fund the purchase of Rangers. Whyte continued to claim that he was using his own personal wealth. In reality, it was a house of cards. Ticketus had paid the £24.4m into an account with Collyer Bristow, Whyte's lawyers during the takeover. Gary Withey of Collyer Bristow, and one of Whyte's first appointments at Rangers, had drafted a letter to Lloyds that claimed the money sitting in this account had been placed there by Whyte himself from his own personal funds.

The news was a pyrrhic victory for the IBC and especially Alastair Johnston and Paul Murray who had sounded the alarm bells before the takeover and had long held suspicions over Whyte's finances. But the deal had gone through. Now Johnston saw only one conceivable outcome – administration. "The club's debts are unsustainable and Octopus [Ticketus] want their money back. It was always his intention to be the guy on the other side of the river when the club came out of administration."

Johnston had never felt that Whyte intended to manage the club over the course of a season. The next step seemed inevitable.

THREE

February 2012 - May 2012

In a round of interviews at the start of February 2012, Whyte continued to assert that the Ticketus money had simply been used to fund a "£10m funding gap" at the club. Yet Whyte had immediately added nearly £4m to the wage bill he inherited – going from £14m to £18m. New contracts, and presumably wage rises, were agreed with Allan McGregor, Steve Davis and Steven Whittaker. McGregor and Davis were certainly key first team players but not many would have said the same about Whittaker. His new contract seemed an unnecessary expense to many supporters. Why was Whyte handing out bumper contracts if he was concerned, as he claimed, about the cost base of the club?

Players had been signed but transfer fees, both in and out, are usually paid in instalments. Lee Wallace, Juan Ortiz, Alejandro Bedoya, Matt McKay, Dorin Goian and Carlos Bocanegra were all signed over the summer for around £3.9m. We know from subsequent events that the fee to Hearts for Wallace was in instalments and Hearts, at this juncture, had received £800,000. That means a total outlay of £3.1m in transfer fees. This needs to be offset by the sale of Madjid Bougherra for £1.8m (believed to be paid in full), £650,000 from the transfer of

Charlie Adam from Blackpool to Liverpool due to a clause inserted in his transfer from Rangers to Blackpool and, finally, Nikica Jelavic had gone to Everton just before the January transfer window closed for a fee believed to be £5m. The club had also taken in over the summer around £3m in outstanding transfer fees from the previous sales of Danny Wilson, Kevin Thomson and Pedro Mendes. Rangers were clearly in the black in their transfer dealings under Whyte and he had inherited a club that had a pre-tax profit.

When Whyte took over, Rangers owed Ticketus around £1.7m to be repaid in May 2011. This was the typical scale of the borrowing Rangers had with Ticketus in their business relationship despite Whyte's claims that he was simply continuing previous arrangements. The club had never required a £30m advance in future season ticket sales simply to get through a season. And we weren't even in February. Warning supporters of "the toughest few weeks in the club's history", it was clear something was afoot.

On February 13, 2012, papers were filed at the Court of Session in Edinburgh signaling the intention of Rangers to go into administration.

In a rambling statement, Whyte made many references to the HMRC tax case as being the trigger for administration, going as far as to claim it could cost the club £75m if it lost. Yet no decision had been reached by the First Tier Tax Tribunal. "If HMRC was to agree, even at this late stage, a manageable agreement with the club then a formal insolvency procedure could yet be averted", he pleaded. Perhaps there is an element of Whyte that genuinely believed this to be a 'tactic' or 'negotiation'. Perhaps he even believed himself to be a brilliant strategist. But there was nothing in his history that would lead HMRC to believe he could ever act in good faith. HMRC had pushed for court appointed administrators, with BDO as their preference, but Lord Menzies accepted Whyte's preference for Duff and Phelps as they had "worked with the club for several months". A partner at Duff and Phelps, David Grier, had walked down Edmiston Drive with Whyte before the first match after his takeover on May 7, 2011.

Despite Whyte's rambling to the contrary, HMRC were not pushing for administration on the grounds of the tax case. In fact, it was because Whyte had not paid VAT or PAYE since September 2011. £5m had been deducted in income tax from employees' wages and not paid and £4m in VAT was unpaid. The club now owed £9m and this was why HMRC had taken the action they did. The big tax case was still undecided.

Having been exposed for not paying VAT or PAYE, Whyte immediately shifted tack into blaming the "existing cost structure of the club". This was the famous '£10m funding gap' again. We've already seen that the club was not in the red from the transfer dealings over the previous nine months. As he'd not paid £9m to HMRC either, he also had this to fall back on. Bear in mind that Whyte's own circular claimed he would put in £5m working capital and £5m on investment in the playing squad. If one was to add up the Ticketus money, season ticket sales, transfer fees, Whyte's own £10m 'investment', hospitality, merchandise income, the club could easily have brought in nearly £60m since the previous May. And he hadn't paid £9m to HMRC either. Not for the first time, Whyte's sums didn't add up.

It was clear that, for Whyte, administration wasn't an unfortunate event caused by unseen escalating costs but a calculated plan that was inevitable from the day he purchased the club. The only unintended event, if there was one, was the failure of the First Tier Tax Tribunal to deliver a verdict, which had been anticipated in the autumn of 2011 but had dragged into 2012.

Alastair Johnston, speaking to the press, warned that "HMRC are not going to lie down and I can tell you, they will have expected this. This will become horribly messy. It will be a horrendous experience for anyone who cares about Rangers Football Club because the club has lost control of its destiny."

A day after administration was confirmed, Paul Murray announced he would put together a consortium called the Blue Knights to try and rescue the club from Whyte's clutches.

Upon the appointment of Duff and Phelps, a Rangers spokesman had anticipated a series of "cost cutting measures" across "all staff levels" as the result of the administration process. This is generally what happens at football clubs. When Motherwell went into administration in 2002, 19 players were immediately made redundant. At Dundee in 2003, 25 staff had gone, including players such as Craig Burley and Fabrizio Ravanelli. None of this happened at Rangers.

In fact, quite the opposite. On the day Rangers lodged papers at the Court of Session on their intention to go into administration, the club also agreed a deal to sign striker Daniel Cousin. Perhaps indicative of how far out of the loop Ally McCoist was in relation to the club's financial position and also indicative of the cavalier nature of the regime. Cousin had played for the club from 2007 to 2008 and was set to return subject to international clearance. In one of the strangest moves of the administration process, Duff and Phelps did not cancel the transfer but, instead, tried to make it happen and were only prevented from completing the transfer by the SPL. There was hardly any pressing football need – not that any supporter was caring too much about football success at this stage. The team was out of the Scottish Cup and, having been four points behind Celtic prior to administration, had been deducted 10 points by the SPL for going into administration. This effectively ended any title race. What desperation there was to sign Cousin on around £7,000 a week when the club was now in administration is unknown.

With great reflexes, on February 17, the SFA launched an inquiry into Rangers after failing to obtain information regarding its "fit and proper person" criteria for club owners. If it wasn't apparent to the SFA by February 2012 that Craig Whyte wasn't a 'fit and proper person' then they really were in trouble. Lord Nimmo Smith would head up the inquiry.

Whyte launched his own pitiful defence of his running of Rangers, going as far as to claim he had not "taken a single penny out of Rangers since I became chairman." This was not true. Within days, it was revealed that the shares Rangers held in Arsenal – and had done so since 1930 – had been sold by Whyte for £230,000. The £230,000 was then transferred, not to Rangers' bank account, but to Pritchard Stockbrokers in Bournemouth – Whyte's own company. Pritchard's assets, as of February 2012, had been frozen by the Financial Services Authority after it was discovered Pritchard had used client money to cover their own costs. If the sale of Rangers' own asset, such as their shares in Arsenal, went to Whyte's company rather than Rangers, how was that not "taking a penny out of the club"?

There were further revelations that £250,000 was paid by Rangers to an amateur football club, Banstead Athletic, which was ran by Aidan Earley, one of Whyte's associates. Why had Rangers paid this money? What were Rangers paying for? What services did Rangers receive? Nothing was apparent.

Duff and Phelps continued. Ali Russell and Gordon Smith were made redundant and Duff and Phelps claimed that the tax debts run up by Whyte since he took over could possibly be £5m more than the £9m they'd previously estimated.

Whyte continued to cost Rangers money and cause problems even while the club was in administration. His failure to disclose his director ban to the PLUS Stock Exchange had led to Rangers' shares being suspended and, on the back of it, the club had been hit with a £50,000 fine. Whyte dismissed the fine as "really irrelevant" which it would be for him as he wouldn't be the one paying it.

Duff and Phelps had been trying to get access to Rangers' client account with Collyer Bristow. In particular, they were trying to get hold of Gary Withey, partner at Collyer Bristow and author of the bogus letter to Lloyds. Duff and Phelps believed there was around £3.6m in this account which belonged to Rangers. They engaged law firm Taylor Wessing to try and make progress on the matter. On the opening day of the case, Mark Phillips QC said "Mr Withey was privy to Mr Whyte's deception and participated in the conspiracy." Withey had said Collyer Bristow was not holding any money, then "changed his story" and said the firm was holding £260,000. Later, another member of staff told administrators that the firm was "in fact holding £3.9m." Where was Gary Withey in all of this? "To use a colloquial expression," said Mark Phillips QC, "Mr Withey 'did a runner'."

The High Court in London agreed that the £3.6m should be moved to a secure account pending a further hearing to establish where it should end up.

On March 2, former Rangers director Hugh Adam gave an interview to the Daily Mail where he claimed Rangers had offered 'side contracts' to players which were not registered with the SFA. There was something grisly and exploitative about the whole thing. Adam was 86 years old and had left the club in 2000, before Rangers had even set up an EBT scheme through the Murray Group. Yet Adam claimed the club had ran such a scheme from the early 1990's. This was not true. Not even this, Adam was never on the board when Rangers ran such a scheme. Adam claimed that the payments were hidden from the public. But the payments were published every year in Rangers accounts so we know that from 2001 to 2010 Rangers paid £47m into Employee Benefit Trusts and paid £500,000 to the Murray Group to manage the scheme. It wasn't just that Adam had a hazy recollection of events; he had no recollection of events as they'd never happened whilst he was there. He even stated that his memory was not what it was – understandably so.

However, the SFA announced it would launch a second inquiry, based on Hugh Adam's claims, and this one would also be chaired by Lord Nimmo Smith. The EBT scheme had been declared in every audited annual account published by Rangers since 2001 and all of those had been lodged at the SFA. If the SFA had an issue then they had taken 11 years to launch an inquiry. Now an inquiry would be launched when the club had no functioning board or any corporate governance at all. When the club needed the Good Samaritan, it got more pocket robbers.

The SFA investigation was compounded by a separate SPL investigation into what it called "undisclosed payments to players." The issue of contracts and what players are paid is clearly a matter for football authorities. One of the main reasons for that is to ensure players are not exploited in any way. Whether or not players had 'undisclosed payments' or 'side contracts', and Rangers denied that they did, it surely could not be argued that the players had been taken advantage of in some way.

In 1992, the STV journalist, Gerry McNee, produced a wage slip on Scotsport which belonged to Duncan Ferguson, then of Dundee United, which showed that Ferguson's £300-a-week wage (with a potential £350 bonus for first-team involvement) had been reduced by a £450 fine, leaving the player penniless. Dubious contracts and fining systems were the order of the day at some clubs. Dundee United's propensity to tie 16-year-olds to '10 year contracts' was a running joke in Scottish football. Several of their players – John Clark, Paddy Connolly, Billy McKinlay - had all sought legal action against the club. Gary Bollan was in the process of taking Dundee United to court in 1995 to invalidate an option United had placed in his contract when he was 17 years old. By a measure of good fortune, Rangers bought Bollan and Alec Cleland for £750,000 and Bollan dropped his court case. This was the kind of player protection that necessitated the registration of contracts.

At the beginning of March, Dave King announced a £20m legal action against former Rangers owner David Murray for "non-disclosure of Rangers true financial position as far back as 2000." King promised to re-invest the money back into Rangers if he was successful. King also met Whyte at this time. He had been informed by Whyte that he was wholly reliant on the Ticketus money and hadn't invested any of his own money into the club. In King's view, this meant the takeover by Whyte had left Rangers in an even worse economic position than before, increasing its indebtedness despite the claims of Whyte and the Murray Group at the time, and one which meant "the club had no chance of survival even if we had progressed in Europe." King believed

Whyte had "duped" the fans and the Murray Group which relied on the proof of funds letter provided by Gary Withey at Collyer Bristow. King concluded that the company would not come out of administration via a Creditors Voluntary Arrangements (CVA) and that "many hurdles will have to be overcome...including having to reapply for membership of the SFA, etc." Since Whyte had first appeared on the scene, King had shown himself to be an astute observer and predictor of events.

Duff and Phelps fired a warning, three weeks after going into the club, that "the club is in a perilous financial situation" and "we can't deliver the cost cuts necessary." It was estimated around £1m a month needed to be saved and the administrators own fees were coming in at around £100,000 a week. There seemed no urgency to get players off the wage bill or to seek dispensation from the authorities to try and secure fees for players. The administrators set a deadline of March 16 for any potential buyers. Eventually, pay cuts of up to 75% were agreed with the players until the end of the season.

Approaching the March deadline, the only obvious buyer in sight was the Blue Knights consortium launched by Paul Murray. Murray had met the administrators and was in the process of putting together his bid. Brian Kennedy, owner of rugby club Sale Sharks, had also expressed an interest but had yet to submit a formal offer and had made it clear he preferred the Blue Knights to take over and saw himself as an option of last resort. The Blue Knights consortium comprised of Paul Murray, Douglas Park, Scott Murdoch and John Bennett. Their plan was to buy the club, submit to a CVA and then proceed to a share issue.

The chances of the Blue Knights succeeding appeared to be given a huge boost when Ticketus said they would lend support to the consortium. Ticketus would not be part of the CVA in return for an agreed restructured payment plan with the Blue Knights for the money they'd loaned Craig Whyte. They would also provide ongoing working capital and credit facilities to the consortium.

With Ticketus seemingly on board, Paul Clark of Duff and Phelps provided more good news that HMRC would, in his view, be willing to agree to a CVA. "HMRC are not saying they are going to be difficult or are going to destroy value. Why would they? It's not in their interests or the taxpayers' interests", he said. The implication being that HMRC would not be an obstacle for any buyer.

The March 16 deadline for buyers saw the Blue Knights, Brian Kennedy, a "Chicago-based consortium called Club 9" and an unnamed UK group all submit formal bids for Rangers. The administrators then extended their deadline seeking "alternative bids" and said they anticipated receiving another one that weekend. It begged the question as to why they bothered setting a deadline in the first place. They promised to have selected two 'preferred bidders' by April 4. The Daily Record reported that the Blue Knights bid was the second largest with the Club 9 bid believed to be the highest.

A blow for the Blue Knights emerged when Craig Whyte told Duff and Phelps that he would not sell his shares to Paul Murray's group under any circumstances. Despite all that had happened, and despite the administrators claims that Whyte's ownership of the shares would not be a problem, Whyte still held his shares in Rangers and any buyer who wished to own the company and put it through a CVA would need to acquire them.

In his revised bid, Paul Murray would agree with Ticketus to repay them £10m over nine years. In return, Ticketus would be removed from the CVA which, in theory, would make any CVA more likely to succeed. Club 9 Sports, the Chicago-based consortium, announced they would not make a revised bid and pulled out of the race.

Former chief executive Martin Bain dropped his legal action at the end of March. The £480,000 that had been frozen in the club's accounts months earlier was now returned to the club minus Bain's legal expenses. With some vindication, Bain pointed out his strong opposition to the Whyte bid "based on investigations into the transparency of his background and the responses to the questions asked of him as part of the process...we asked him businesslike questions regarding the cashflow of the club and his ability to fund the club going forward." Bain pointed out that net debt had fallen from £31m in June 2009 to £14m in June 2011 whilst turnover had increased. How much of this was down to the board and how much was down to Walter Smith is open to debate. But it was always worth pointing out that Whyte had not taken over an economic basket case but had, in fact, created one.

Duff and Phelps launched a "professional negligence" claim of £25m against Collyer Bristow at the High Court in London. The case would be settled out of court two years later. On the April 4 deadline for revised bids, the administrators confirmed they had received four bids – the Blue Knights and bids from the US, Singapore and Germany. Like Club 9, Brian Kennedy had chosen not to submit a revised bid but remained open to coming in as a bidder of last resort.

In early April, the administrators published a report of all creditors. HMRC topped the list with a claim of £93m. Yet the bulk of this was made up of £75m from the tax case that was awaiting a tribunal verdict. Quite why HMRC were able to claimed to be owed money that had not been agreed was owed was a surprise to the layperson. Even if some money was owed, where had the £75m figure come from? The rest was made up of £14m of PAYE and VAT that

Whyte had not paid plus £4m from the smaller tax case which Whyte was also meant to have paid. Ticketus were the second biggest creditor at £26.7m. It added up to a headline grabbing figure of £140m, the majority of which comprised of the disputed £75m to HMRC and the £26.7m to Ticketus which Whyte had borrowed and dumped on the club to make it 'debt free'.

Two other bidders for the club went public in April. Bill Miller, an American businessman who had been involved in the Club 9 bid, and Bill Ng, a businessman based in Singapore.

By now, the possibility of a 'newco' scenario was being floated by Duff and Phelps, by Bill Miller (it was his preferred option) and the media. The difficulties of Whyte's shares, and extracting them from him, along with the HMRC claims made the possibility of moving the assets to a new company more and more tempting.

But, of course, it's never that simple. The possibility of a 'newco' scenario prompted the SPL to urgently revisit their rules regarding clubs suffering insolvency events and, in particular, the prospect of a 'newco' club – where a club transfers its SPL share to a new company. The proposals included an increase in punishment for entering administration from 10 points to 15 points or a third of the previous season's total, whichever was the greater. There was also a proposal to deduct 75% of

SPL income from 'newco' clubs for three years, on top of the points deduction

Neil Doncaster struck a conciliatory note that any penalties would only apply for transfers that happened after May 15 thus Duff and Phelps and any potential buyer had that time to get the process sorted, if that was their preferred option. Doncaster also observed that the 'newco' scenario, whilst untried in Scotland, had been used in England and Plymouth Argyle and Crystal Palace, among others, had used that process to exit administration without any penalty from the English authorities. The process, at this stage, still required only the SPL board to approve the transfer of the SPL share. The board comprised chairman Ralph Topping, Neil Doncaster, Stephen Thompson (Dundee United), Derek Weir (Motherwell), Steven Brown (St Johnstone) and Eric Riley (Celtic).

On April 16, the Blue Knights announced that they were stepping back from the bid after it was revealed Ticketus, which had been part of their consortium, was now in negotiations with Bill Ng's group. The Blue Knights had offered £10m over nine years to Ticketus in return for their co-operation. Perhaps inevitably, this was trumped by another bidder. In this case, Ng offered Ticketus £14m over a shorter period. Prior to this development, the Blue Knights had believed they were about to be named preferred bidders by Duff and Phelps. The administrators had requested a non-refundable exclusivity fee of £500,000. Ticketus did not wish to provide it.

Two months into the administration and the process was starting to resemble a long-running West End farce. Following on from the Blue Knights announcement, Brian Kennedy re-emerged and stated his intention to re-enter the race. It then appeared that Bill Miller, who had been written off, was the new front runner for a few hours. And then, to top it all, Bill Ng was unable to reach an agreement with Ticketus. This was the final straw for Ng who then withdrew from the race also citing his belief that Duff and Phelps would not be able to deliver on Craig Whyte's shares.

In the public domain, as of April 20, this left only three bidders – the Blue Knights, Brian Kennedy and Bill Miller. The offer submitted by the Blue Knights at the start of April was still on the table. Bill Miller's plans were what he called an 'incubator' company. Duff and Phelps would take the club through a CVA whilst Miller moved the assets into an 'incubator' company. Or, as he rather poetically described it, "I will put the heart of the club into an 'incubator' company while Duff & Phelps work to make the sick patient healthy through a CVA process that effectively works to radiate the toxicity of past administrations' sins out of the patient while the healthy heart is preserved and moves forward." Miller would then acquire the plc from the administrators after the CVA process was completed, reuniting 'patient' and 'heart'. Miller's offer, however, was also contingent on a guarantee from the SPL and SFA that Rangers would play in the SPL in 2012-13 with no points deductions or removal of trophies.

Brian Kennedy had made a revised verbal offer to Duff and Phelps – "a double-digit million-pound bid", as he described it – but this had been rejected immediately. The position of the Blue Knights at this stage was uncertain.

The position of Craig Whyte's shares and how to get them had been the obstacle for Ng, was a potential issue for the Blue Knights and possibly Brian Kennedy. Bill Miller believed he could circumvent the need for Whyte's shares with his 'incubator' idea. It was revealed that, in discussions with Ticketus regarding his shares, Whyte was demanding two seats in the directors' box at Ibrox for the rest of his life, a 20% stake in the club and the ability to appoint two directors onto the next board.

The SFA inquiry that had begun in February just days after the club entered administration, delivered its verdict at the end of April. The club was found guilty by an SFA Judicial Panel of bringing the game into disrepute, was hit with fines totaling £160,000 and, most severely of all, received a 12-month ban on signing players. Craig Whyte was fined £200,000 and banned from holding office in

Scottish football for life. The Panel was made up of Gary Allan QC, Eric Drysdale (Raith Rovers) and former football commentator, Alastair Murning. The administrators had tried to defend the club over the three-day hearing. In trying to demonstrate the distinction between the individual and the club, they had produced evidence to show that Whyte had abandoned any form of corporate governance at the club, was unaccountable to anyone at the club and that all decisions were taken solely by him.

The transfer embargo was especially difficult for a club that, irrespective of what may happen over the next few weeks, was always going to require a major overhaul of its playing squad over the upcoming summer. In essence, the club was to lose players due to administration and then not to be allowed to replace them. Duff and Phelps, representing the club, launched an appeal. The appeal would be funded by the Rangers Fans Fighting Fund. Launched in February to receive donations from supporters to help the club, it had around £500,000. The appeal would be conducted by Richard Keen QC, the Dean of the Faculty of Advocates.

By the end of April, there were only two formal offers on the table for the club. A joint bid from Blue Knights and Brian Kennedy for £5m and Bill Miller's 'incubator' proposal. Ticketus were no longer part of the Blue Knights proposal and both they and Miller also proposed removing the Rangers bond holders from the CVA, a move worth around

£8m. There would be an initial cash payment and then a series of instalments giving an eventual total of £10m. The Blue Knights also committed to paying the football debts, believed to be around £3m. Unfortunately, Whyte had already indicated his refusal to deal with the Blue Knights so Paul Murray was now relying on goodwill. Despite attempts by Brian Kennedy and Ticketus to appeal to Whyte's better nature, if such a thing existed, it was not forthcoming.

On May 3, Bill Miller was named the preferred bidder. Miller's bid was worth £11.2m and would involve the creation of a 'newco' to take the club, players, stadium, SPL membership and separate it from the tax issues which would reside with RFC plc. RFC plc would go through a CVA and, if successful, would then take the 'newco' back under its wing. The downsides for this scheme were many. The club would be banned from European football for three years due to the formation of a 'newco'. Craig Whyte's shares in RFC plc would be almost worthless whilst the CVA process was underway but, if that was successful, and it was merged with 'newco', then they would go up in value. He would retain his stake. It seemed very complicated and nor did it seem likely that Miller could do all this without working with Whyte, despite claiming he wouldn't. Yet Miller seemed sincere, despite supporter opposition to the plan, and Duff and Phelps even claimed HMRC supported his bid.

Responding to this, the Blue Knights expressed their disappointment and said Miller's proposal would have "long term financial consequences" for Rangers. They also expressed their frustration that while the Whyte shares issue had always been there as an uncertainty, "it is only in recent days this issue has been seen as an impediment to overcome in enabling us to make an unconditional CVA offer to Duff and Phelps."

Bill Miller withdrew his bid on May 8 blaming supporter hostility. It was difficult to see what had dramatically changed in that regard in the space of a week. On the same day, The Sun ran with the story that Craig Whyte had struck a deal over his shares with a UK consortium. This prompted Brian Kennedy and Paul Murray to have one final attempt. They had thought their bid had been accepted the previous week only for Duff and Phelps to say they couldn't deliver Whyte's shares. Duff and Phelps then appointed Bill Miller as preferred bidder whilst denying they'd ever accepted the Blue Knights bid. We were nearly three months into the administration process.

On May 12, the SFA released the detailed judgement behind their Judicial Panel's decision. It wrote "The question might be, "What could they do?" 'The answer is, "They could have made public the activities of Mr Craig Whyte of which they were aware or ought to have been aware".' Forms requested by the SFA regarding their 'fit and proper' test were signed off by Whyte's friend, Gary Withey, rather than the head of football administration at Rangers, Andrew Dickson. The financial controller, Ken Olverman, was told to report only to Craig Whyte and to refuse a request for financial information from Dave King. From September 19, 2011, Olverman was instructed not to pay NI, PAYE and VAT. This, Whyte had told Olverman, was indeed one of his brilliant "negotiating tactics" with HMRC. £13m would be withheld from September 2011 to February 2012. Nor did the financial controller know anything about Ticketus. There had been no money from Ticketus into Rangers' bank account. The only transfers from Collyer Bristow to Rangers were £200,000 in mid-November, when Olverman was concerned the club was running out of money and £800,000 a month later when Olverman expressed doubts about the ability to pay that month's wage bill. The tribunal's own report states that 'in all material respects, between 6 May 2011 and 14 February 2012, Mr Craig Whyte was "the directing mind and will" of Rangers FC.'

It was difficult to understand. The tribunal decided that the suspicions of Dave King, John McClelland and John Greig about Whyte's running of the club and the financial situation were worthy of punishment rather than evidence that corporate governance at the club had completely broken down and that key personnel were cut off from decision making. McClelland and Greig had both resigned in

October because they were "being excluded from participating in corporate governance at the club". King had been vocal since May 2011 that the Whyte takeover was a bad one and had warned several times in public that he saw administration as inevitable. He'd also been denied access to financial information. What were those board members meant to do? Report it to the football authorities? We know that the SFA were aware that Whyte was not paying PAYE or VAT in October 2011. The tribunal seemed to be arguing that Rangers directors should have done more, like reporting Whyte to the game's authorities who already knew anyway but did nothing. It seemed the height of absurdity.

Incredibly, the tribunal had looked at the possibility of termination of membership of the SFA as a punishment but considered this as "too severe."

The Blue Knights withdrew their £11m bid for the club on the same day that Charles Green and his consortium were expected to be given preferred bidder status. Green's offer was said to be made up of £5.5m up front, £3.5m for debts and £2m conditional on European football in seasons two and three.

It had been a long year since Whyte took over the previous May and it was not about to get much better.

FOUR

May 2012 - August 2012

Eighty-eight days after entering administration, Duff and Phelps agreed a deal to sell Rangers to a consortium led by Charles Green. Green had been chief executive at Sheffield United 16 years earlier. He said he had bought Whyte's shares from him for £1 - an unusually low figure from a man not given to acts of charity. What could possibly be in it for Whyte?

His plan, as announced at his opening press conference, was to submit a CVA on June 6 for £8.5m. If this failed, he would go down the 'newco' route. He had already registered a company called 'Sevco 5088 Ltd' on March 29. Green had never spoken publicly about his move for Rangers prior to May 13, nor had Duff and Phelps ever mentioned him as one of the bidders. Green certainly had no obligation to conduct his business in public but one would have thought the administrators may have been a little more transparent.

The appeal against the 12-month transfer embargo was rejected in the middle of May by a panel chaired by Lord Carloway with Spartans chairman Craig

Graham and former Partick Thistle chairman Allan Cowan also on the panel. The legal advice received by Duff and Phelps was that the sanction was not "competent" and had not been a sanction available to the original tribunal. The matter would be appealed to the courts.

Having failed to gain control of the club via any of the consortiums vying for power, Ticketus said they would not oppose any CVA. Instead, they would focus their efforts on reclaiming their money from Craig Whyte himself who, lest we forget, had made personal and corporate guarantees to Ticketus.

On May 23, BBC Scotland ran another documentary on Rangers entitled 'The Men Who Sold The Jerseys.' The documentary alleged that David Grier, of Duff and Phelps, knew that Craig Whyte was using Ticketus to fund his takeover. Grier denied this, saying "it wasn't in our terms of engagement." Gary Withey, of Collyer Bristow, had sent an email to Whyte and Grier on April 19, 2011 entitled 'Ticketus draft' stating that when Whyte takes control "the assignation documents will be released by the bank and the Ticketus agreements will become unconditional".

Duff and Phelps had taken legal action against Collyer Bristow on the basis that the law firm had failed to declare prior to the takeover that the source of funding was Ticketus, and not Whyte. Grier denied any knowledge that funds of Ticketus were being used prior to the takeover. He said Ticketus had been discussed with Whyte but only as a short-term source of working capital.

Grier and the Rangers administrators David Whitehouse and Paul Clark were part of a company called MCR which was bought over by Duff & Phelps. Paul Clark stated that "MCR became aware of the full scale of Ticketus funding in July or August. There is a world of difference between knowing that Ticketus was a potential source of working capital funding for the club... and knowing that funding from ticket sales had been effectively used to purchase the club."

The documentary also fleshed out the EBT scheme that was subject to the tax dispute with HMRC. A total of £47.659m from 2001 to 2010 was paid to the Murray Group Remuneration Trust which was based in Jersey. The trust would then divide this into separate sub-trusts for players and staff to access as tax-free loans. A total of 63 players and 24 staff at Rangers were involved in the scheme with an additional 24 Murray Group employees also involved. Employees could borrow money from the trusts which could, in theory, be repaid at the request of the trustees. The position of HMRC was that these loans would, in practice, never be repaid and, therefore, constituted income and should be subject to income tax. The position of the Murray Group was they were loans, not income, and were not a contractual entitlement. The biggest trust belonged to David Murray himself who had received £6.3m over the years. Around £11m in total had went to non-playing staff.

In the latest appeal against the 12-month transfer embargo, the administrators took the SFA to the Court of Session in Edinburgh. Richard Keen QC was again funded by the Rangers Fans Fighting Fund and the position of the administrators remained that the punishment was not available to the panel. Lord Glennie at the Court of Session agreed that the ban was 'improper' and that the panel should have looked at the punishments available and not simply made one up. The SFA elected not to appeal and referred the case back to the Tribunal.

On May 29, Charles Green published his CVA proposal that would go to a creditor vote on June 14. There were some surprising details. Green proposed a total of £8.5m to all creditors. This £8.5m, however, would be in the form of a loan that Rangers would pay back to his consortium by, or before, 2020 at an interest rate of 8%. Green had claimed Rangers would never be in debt again under his watch and yet, just days later, he was proposing to land the club with millions of pounds of debt should it exit administration via a CVA.

There were other issues. The loan provided by Green would not be available until mid-July. How would the club's running costs be met until then? Duff and Phelps fees alone were £3m at this stage and there was a further £1.8m in legal fees. Duff and Phelps had requested that all bidders provide funding from June 1 over and above any offer they wished to make. Yet Green's consortium did not do so. His £3.6m Administration Trading Shortfall is included in the CVA proposal. Creditors would pay for the running costs of the club. Nor did Duff and Phelps know all the members of Green's consortium. Asked to provide £2.7m as the first down payment on his purchase, Green had only been able to offer £1m. The twenty investors that he had originally claimed had shrunk to 'around six'. The CVA did not allow for any future incentive for creditors either through a slice of TV money, prize money or European income – generally accepted as a crucial factor in securing the vote of HMRC.

If the CVA failed, Green had a binding agreement with Duff and Phelps that he would be able to purchase all of the assets of the club for a fixed price of £5.5m. There was a school of thought, not unreasonable, that the assets of Rangers would have fetched much higher than £5.5m in an open market.

The admittance of the tax case, that was under dispute, into the CVA also meant that any payment to all creditors would be delayed until that verdict was delivered. In addition, Duff and Phelps legal case against Collyer Bristow also had to be settled. Creditors would be asked to vote but not know how much or when they will receive it. It was a big ask. The proposal lacked certainty, to say the least. It was hard to accept that this was the most attractive option available since February.

At the start of June, an email exchange between Craig Whyte and David Grier was made public. Whyte had emailed Grier on February 11 requesting that there be "no unpleasant surprises" in the administration process, that it should be "short…preferably in hours" and costs kept to a maximum of £500,000. Grier replied agreeing to a short process and to cap costs at £500,000. Duff and Phelps accused the BBC, which had published the emails, of "misrepresenting our position." The costs and timeframe provided to Whyte in the emails, said Paul Clark of Duff and Phelps, were only "estimates" and "based on a specific possible outcome."

On June 14, the CVA was formally rejected. HMRC cited their policy of not agreeing to a CVA where "there is historical non-compliance by a company with tax liabilities." However, the tax case was under dispute and HMRC themselves had only presented Rangers with their claim retrospectively, in 2010. Whyte's willful non-payment of PAYE and VAT was over five months. It was hardly proof of some historical, institutional problem. Nor was it clear why Duff and Phelps had made optimistic noises throughout the process about HMRC's co-operation if HMRC had a long-standing policy that meant they would always reject any CVA.

The HMRC rejection was also sold as allowing them to launch an investigation into Craig Whyte's running of the company. There were three other rejections, one of which was Rapid Vienna, owed around £1m for striker Nikica Jelavic.

BDO were to be liquidators and the sales of the company's assets to Charles Green's 'newco' would be completed later that day. Malcolm Murray would be appointed chairman of the 'newco' with Charles Green as chief executive. Imran Ahmad would be commercial director and Brian Stockbridge would be finance director.

The players had agreed pay cuts with the administrators in April. The pay cuts had ended on June 1 when the players reverted to their normal terms and conditions. The expectation was that the players would transfer under TUPE regulations. The Transfer of Undertakings (Protection of Employment) regulations exist primarily to protect employees and their terms and conditions with the new employer. They are generally supported by trade unions.

PFA Scotland, however, had been agitating in the press since April that the players would, if they chose, be free agents and the chief executive of PFA Scotland, Fraser Wishart, said the administrators had been told this was the union's position. It's unusual to see a trade union arguing that their members should be made unemployed. A hardened cynic might argue that some players saw the opportunity to pocket a larger than usual signing on fee, in the absence of any transfer fee. However, this is idle speculation.

Sone Aluko and Rhys McCabe were the first two players to signal their intention to leave. This was followed by the now notorious departure of Steven Whittaker and Steven Naismith. Naismith would join Everton and subsequently Norwich City for a fee believed to be around £8m. This was the kind of money that some of these players commanded in an open transfer market. One wonders what Rangers could have done with that money, or something close to it, long before the TUPE saga unfolded.

In the end, 18 players would stay, including Lee McCulloch, Lee Wallace, Barrie McKay, Lewis MacLeod, Neil Alexander and Kyle Hutton. Maurice Edu agreed to the TUPE transfer so that Rangers would receive a fee from Stoke City. Rangers also agreed fees with Southampton, Sheffield Wednesday and Coventry City for Steve Davis, Rhys McCabe and John Fleck.

Rather than letting sleeping dogs lie, PFA Scotland then launched, in December 2012, an employment tribunal claim on behalf, they said, of 67 players. Lee McCulloch immediately tweeted that he had not given his consent for the move and would be asking for his name to be removed. Nor had the 18 players who had agreed to TUPE over. Nor, it turned out, had Aluko. Or Allan McGregor. The tenacity of the PFA in this was odd.

The day after the CVA was rejected, Walter Smith announced he would lead a consortium involving billionaire Jim McColl and Douglas Park to purchase the club from Green.

On June 25, the Crown Office announced that it had "instructed Strathclyde Police to conduct a criminal investigation into the acquisition of Rangers Football Club in May 2011 and the subsequent financial management of the club. The investigation into alleged criminality follows a preliminary police examination of information passed to them in February this year by the club administrators. The Procurator Fiscal for the West of Scotland will now work with Strathclyde Police to fully investigate the acquisition and financial management of Rangers Football Club and any related reports of alleged criminality during that process."

The transfer of Rangers' SPL share required the approval of the majority of SPL clubs. They would meet at the end of June to make the decision. A stranger watching the reaction to this situation might have formed the opinion that Scottish football had, hitherto, been a place of financial probity, good governance and sound ownership. They would not have formed the impression that Rangers had been subject to a dubious takeover and ran deliberately into administration.

Yet a number of clubs had either experienced financial distress or come perilously close it. Dundee had entered administration twice, in 2003 and 2010, as had Livingston, in 2004 and 2009. Motherwell had entered administration in 2002. Some of the biggest sanctimony came from clubs who had encountered their own problems in the past with financial difficulty or mismanagement or those who would soon have them in the future.

'Sporting integrity' staggered back onto the scene in 2012 and with even less credibility than it had in 2008. Clubs that had dodged relegation on technicalities or played fast and loose with the authorities suddenly found themselves on a slippery moral high ground.

Aberdeen had finished bottom of the league in 2000 but were spared relegation because Falkirk, the First Division champions, did not have enough seats in their stadium. Motherwell had twice avoided relegation in 1986 and 2003 due to league reconstruction – the second time in the middle of their administration process which lasted two years. St. Mirren had avoided relegation in 1991 for the same reason. The supporters of those clubs fizzed at the mouth about 'sporting integrity'.

John Yorkston, the chairman of Dunfermline Athletic, said that Dunfermline could have spent £2m on players rather than taxes and, therefore, he reasoned, avoided relegation. "We chose to pay the taxman", he said. He doth protest too much. Within months, Dunfermline would go into administration owing HMRC unpaid tax.

One of the biggest noises came from Hearts. Hearts had been run by a Lithuanian owner, Vladimir Romanov, since 2005. Romanov had piled millions of pounds of debt onto the Tynecastle club in that period. Leading up to 2012, Hearts had their own issues with HMRC. In February 2012, they faced their third winding-up order from HMRC in six months and this following on from a period of non-payment of wages to players. One of their players, Ryan Stevenson, had went on strike over not being paid.

And yet, it was against this backdrop, that Romanov belched to the Hearts website about Rangers being part of a "Scottish football mafia" that had "plotted to push Hearts into bankruptcy". Unfortunately, for Hearts fans, Hearts did not need any pushing. Romanov was doing a perfectly good job of it by himself.

Hearts would enter administration in June 2013 with debts of £30m (2012 turnover: £6.9m). A month earlier, Romanov's company, and Hearts parent company, UBIG, had been declared bankrupt. Bizarrely, the SPL did not consider this as 'an insolvency event' and, therefore, did not levy Hearts with the 18-point deduction that would have relegated Hearts in 2013. Generously, the SPL waited a month before applying a 15-point deduction which allowed Hearts to start the 2013-14 season in the SPL minus 15 points.

There was speculation that political pressure may be placed on the Lithuanian authorities during Hearts administration. The First Minister of Scotland at the time was Alex Salmond, a proven Hearts supporter. He had promised no political interference and that's what happened.

Fortunately, the Lithuanian savers of UBIG were in a benevolent mood and wrote off nearly £28m. Perhaps they just liked Hearts. In the end, Hearts would repay £2.5m of the £30m they owed. Romanov claimed asylum in Moscow and is still wanted by Interpol and the Lithuanian authorities on charges of fraud, embezzlement and money laundering. Hearts would later be held up by the Scottish media as an example of a model football club.

In the end, the clubs voted 10-1 against allowing the share transfer – Rangers had naturally voted for it. Kilmarnock abstained. Green claimed he'd asked the SPL if the application should be withdrawn beforehand given the level of reported opposition. He claimed the SPL told him that it "still stood a chance of success." Perhaps they enjoyed watching the dance.

This high-minded finger-wagging from the SPL clubs was not entirely principled. They were not going to vote for the transfer of Rangers' SPL share. But they certainly did not want to be without

Rangers for too long. That might be ridiculous and cost too much money. Instead, the SPL hatched a plan to demand that the Scottish Football League accept Rangers into the First Division. The theory being that Rangers would be out of the top division for one year only and the rest of the league could go back to their moral superiority once the money was rolling in again.

The SPL and the SFA set about trying a mixture of blackmail and cajoling to get the SFL clubs to accept Rangers into the First Division. Clubs were threatened that it would lead to a "financial meltdown". The £2m annual settlement paid by the SPL to the SFL was said to be at risk. Placing Rangers in the Third Division, the SFL was warned, would cost Scottish football £16m. The SFL clubs were offered a 'merger', an SPL2, league reconstruction that would involve play-offs between the leagues, a 16-team league by 2014 in a new three division set-up, improved money in the long-term and an additional £1m to the First Division clubs in television money.

Television money was one of the big prizes at stake. The SPL had lucrative deals with Sky and ESPN. But these deals were signed on the understanding that Rangers would be in the top flight and would carry the burden of the majority of live TV fixtures. These agreements would now have to be rewritten, at substantial cost to the SPL. They needed the agreement of the SFL to show Rangers' matches.

The blackmail wasn't restricted simply to SFL clubs. In return for the dubious prize of playing in the Scottish First Division, the SPL and SFA wanted Rangers to be stripped of the league titles won in 2003, 2005, 2009, 2010 and 2011 and the Scottish Cups won in 2002, 2003, 2008 and 2009. The plan also included stripping the Scottish League Cups won by Rangers in 2002, 2003, 2005, 2008 and 2010 but the Scottish Football League refused to participate in the sham proceedings. It was testament to those involved in the SFL that they saw straight through the proposals and identified them as nothing more than a witch-hunt that went against even a basic notion of presumption of innocence. Rangers would also be required to accept the one-year transfer embargo imposed by the SFA which had been overturned by the Court of Session. The transfer embargo was a moot point as Rangers had not been able to sign anyone that summer in any case due to the ongoing uncertainty and turmoil. But the loss of trophies fairly won was without precedent in world football. It was a scandalous proposal.

In Stalin's USSR, people were airbrushed from photographs, removed from the history books as they fell out of favour with the leader or the historical record had to be changed to reflect what the leader wanted today.

This was Scottish football's attempt at Stalin's Photoshop. To remake the images of the past and rewrite the historical record to reflect what the owners of the present wanted it to say. "Do you remember the last day title shoot-out of 2003? No, you don't, as it didn't happen. Do you remember Helicopter Sunday when the league was won in the last minute? What are you talking about, comrade? That never happened. Do you want to get us both into trouble?"

In Italy, Juventus, AC Milan, Fiorentina, Lazio and Reggina had been found guilty of match fixing by influencing and selecting favourable referees. All five clubs received points deductions. Juventus were also stripped of the 2004-05 Serie A title that they'd won and they were consigned to the bottom of Serie A in 2005-06, handing the title to Inter Milan, and relegating Juventus to Serie B. The 2005 title was not assigned to the runner-up. In France, Bernard Tapie's Marseille were stripped of their 1993 French title over allegations of match fixing. This too was not assigned to the runner-up. They retained the 1993 UEFA Champions League but were not allowed to defend it in 1993-94.

These were cases of actual match fixing where the result had been influenced by corruption, bribery of officials or opposition. It was impossible to see the comparison with Rangers' situation. If the view was that the use of a tax avoidance scheme was so serious that it rendered bribery then any manner of player perks was open to similar dubious interpretation. A club car? Players paid separately for image rights? Flights back home? Accommodation for family?

As yet, the tax tribunal had not even agreed that any tax was due. If the mere use of them was 'morally wrong' then why hadn't Celtic been punished for using one for Juninho in 2004-05? If the issue was that they'd been used but the tax had not been paid then, as said, no tax amount had even been agreed yet. It did not appear that Rangers were guilty of anything other than being subject to a dubious takeover and then not having a CVA accepted. There was a presumption of guilt and to deliver a punishment, a disproportionate one at that, before anything had been established.

The authorities miscalculated Rangers' desperation to play in the Scottish First Division. The support and the manager were not keen to do so. It's possible that Charles Green, left to his own devices, may well have signed up but even he, too, was adamant, in public at any rate, that he could not countenance such a move.

Asked by the Daily Mail the night before the vote, only two clubs, Stenhousemuir and Brechin City, publicly supported Rangers going into the First Division.

On July 13, the matter was put to a vote. Of the 30 SFL clubs, 25 voted against the proposal and, instead, agreed that Rangers should join the league in the Third Division. The meeting had been addressed by Ally McCoist and Charles Green. McCoist openly favoured Rangers going into the Third Division as did the majority of Rangers fans. Raith Rovers chairman Turnbull Hutton had called the attempt to force the SFL to place Rangers into the First Division as "corruption". Whoever was corrupt in that scenario, it certainly wasn't Rangers.

The issue of stealing trophies from Rangers was not completely off the table either. The SFA had commissioned Lord Nimmo Smith to investigate whether any rules had been broken regarding player registrations and the issue of 'dual contracts'.

The bid by Walter Smith's consortium failed to persuade Charles Green and his consortium to sell up. It had been too little, too late. McColl had now dipped his toe in Rangers' waters a couple of times but had said he could never get fully involved due to time demanded of his other investments.

Rangers' prize money for 2011-12, for finishing second, was £900,000. The SPL decided to withhold this. Southampton had agreed to pay £800,000 for Steven Davis. Davis had refused to sign terms with Southampton unless they made an offer of payment. The FA requested that the fee be sent to the SFA and not Rangers.

A compromise was reached with the SFA over the transfer embargo on July 20. In return for the transfer of SFA membership to the newco, Rangers would accept the transfer ban but its implementation would be delayed until September 1, giving Rangers around six weeks to replace the multi-million pounds squad of internationalists that had just walked out the door for nothing. The club also agreed, not unreasonably, to settle all outstanding football debts.

The SFL had sensed its strong hand in respect to having Rangers in the lower leagues and the desire for TV companies to show their games live. The SFL was a separate body from the SPL so was not tied to the Sky and ESPN contracts that they had. Rather than hand over the rights, the SFL employed IMG to seek interested parties for the package of 44 live Rangers matches for the next three seasons.

It is unsurprising, then, that the SPL bid for the rights. They offered £1.2m – an average of £27,000 a game. It was a paltry sum and, unfortunately, Rangers, as mere associate members of the SFL, had no influence on the deal. Nor would they be able to influence the SPL's frantic renegotiations with Sky and ESPN which hinged on the SPL securing rights to Rangers' matches. Rangers were to be shown every other week and their supporters were expected to pick up the majority of TV sports subscriptions. But they would have no voice and crumbs from the table as a reward.

On July 27, the SFA confirmed the transfer of membership to the newco. This would allow Rangers to kickstart their season at Brechin in the Ramsdens Cup two days later.

It had been a traumatic summer and the club had not received much in the way of political or media support for their plight. One MSP, John Mason (SNP), said that he thought it would be good for his team, Clyde FC, for Rangers to play in the lower leagues due to the financial benefits of a large Rangers away support. This was like stating it was good for an innocent man to go to jail because it helped to keep prison officers in their jobs. Mason would subsequently go on to state that he considered the use of tax vehicles to reduce tax burden as morally worse than the sexual abuse of children. Mason was an accountant before lending his intellect to the political world. The accountancy world's loss had been politics loss.

Mason was typical of the modern politician in Scotland. Small-minded but with a disproportionately high opinion of himself. Mason was considered a crank, even within his own party, and could be just as comfortable thundering against gay marriage. Sticking the boot into Rangers was an easy way for many to balance the scales, win some kudos and appear progressive.

The club had been subject to a fraudulent takeover 15 months earlier and placed into administration by willfully reckless mismanagement. The club had been fined, docked points, received a transfer ban, lost £20m+ worth of players for free, had prize money withheld, was subject to two separate investigations by the SFA and SPL, had their TV rights handed over to prop up the SPL's TV deal, been threatened with losing nine trophies in exchange for being relegated and simply to benefit the SPL and now, finally, was being allowed to play in the Scottish Third Division. It had been an unsavoury free-for-all. And yet some would say Rangers hadn't been punished at all.

FIVE

August 2012 - May 2013

One of the conditions of Rangers' SFA membership transfer was the payment of all football debts. The SFA had received £800,000 from Southampton for the transfer of Steve Davis. Charles Green, not unreasonably, assumed that the SFA would pay Dundee United the £31,000 they were owed from this. The SFA said Rangers should pay it. It seemed that the SFA and SPL wanted Rangers to pay the football debts and also hand over any football money that was due to them.

The league season had begun at Balmoor in Peterhead. Barrie McKay outpaced the part-timers to give Rangers an early lead. In the second half, though, Peterhead turned things around to put themselves 2-1 in front. A scrambled last minute equaliser spared Rangers' blushes. It wasn't the start anyone had imagined. Promotion would be clinched but there would be such hiccups along the way. Talk of going unbeaten throughout the league season soon ended.

Progress had been made in the League Cup against East Fife, Falkirk and a rousing victory over Motherwell at Ibrox. In the summer, the Motherwell support had behaved with all the restraint and wisdom of a stone-throwing mob in the Life of Brian. Now every match felt like a grudge match as relationships between Rangers and almost all of Scottish football had broken down. Revenge had been sweet. The adrenalin of the Motherwell match was absent a month later in the competition as Rangers succumbed to top-flight Inverness Caley Thistle. It was becoming obvious that bridging the gap of playing part-time teams in the league then top-flight sides in cup competitions wasn't going to be as easily done as first anticipated.

Interest in the Scottish Cup was ended with a defeat at Tannadice to Dundee United. Rangers had refused to take tickets for the match. Prompted by supporter groups, the club had agreed to an official boycott. United had been unsympathetic, to say the least, towards Rangers in the summer. But there were other issues. In 2009, a match between Dundee United and Rangers at Tannadice had been abandoned. Dundee United refused to issue refunds to the travelling Rangers support and insisted on charging £12 to enter the re-arranged match.

Dundee United complained to the SFA and requested the right to keep all the gate money from the Cup tie for themselves. An interesting proposal from a club that had often brought a handful of supporters to Glasgow and accepted their half of the gate money. Their request was denied. Unfortunately, around 400 Rangers supporters defied the club's request not to attend.

At the end of August, Duff and Phelps revealed their latest update on fees accrued throughout the administration process. The bill for six months work came to £3.1m with an additional £104,000 for proposing the CVA. Lawyers Biggart Baillie were paid £50,000 for placing Rangers into administration. PR firm Media House received £112,500 and a media consultancy group called Spreckley were paid £28,941. Duff and Phelps had recovered £111,607 from Pritchard Stockbrokers who had received the funds from the sale of Arsenal shares that Rangers owned. Duff and Phelps had claimed for the full £223,214 but Pritchard were now in administration so full recovery was unlikely. UEFA also owed Rangers money from international appearances by their players and £800,000 in transfer fees.

Charles Green had refused to co-operate with the SPL investigation into dual contracts issue. Green claimed the SPL had been made aware of the EBT issue in dialogue with HMRC in October 2010 but had done nothing. In reality, the SPL had known about the scheme since 2001 and had done nothing. It was clear, too, from the 'offer' to remove nine trophies from Rangers that the club could make the whole inquiry go away if they had just accepted this outrageous proposal. It wasn't quite like something from The Godfather but it is no surprise that Green retained scepticism about the nature of the inquiry from the start.

It was claimed, from an SPL source, that they had not investigated Celtic's use of an EBT with Juninho in 2005 because the player had been paid after he'd left Celtic. The payment had not been disclosed to the SPL or SFA but was disclosed in the club's annual accounts. It was difficult to see what difference this was from their use by Rangers. Apparently, the fact Juninho had left Celtic and received money was different from receiving money whilst playing for them. Or something.

In October, Craig Whyte resurfaced in an interview with the BBC. He claimed to have introduced Charles Green to Duff and Phelps. It is undeniably true that Green would have had conversations with Whyte. Anyone looking to take the club through the CVA process needed Whyte's shares. Whyte had already refused to sell to the Blue Knights. In a statement on the Rangers website, Green claimed it was "misleading" to say he was brought in by Craig Whyte. Green claimed to have been brought to the table by Zeus Capital's Imran Ahmad, now on the board at Rangers. He said Duff and Phelps had made the initial contact with Zeus Capital. Green's version of Whyte's demands - £1m a season, seats in the director's box for life - were certainly familiar.

Whyte's version of events was that he used his "contacts in the city" to find a suitable buyer. He also claimed Duff and Phelps knew about the Ticketus deal from the start. This was denied by Paul Clark of Duff and Phelps who called the allegations "false, malicious and without foundation." Whyte also claimed not to have lied to the support when he said season tickets weren't mortgaged because, technically, they had not been 'mortgaged'. They had been leveraged. So that's alright, then.

Whyte moaned that Duff and Phelps had reneged on a deal to perform a quick administration for a capped fee of £500,000. Whyte intended to get Rangers in and out of administration as quickly as possible. How he would negotiate the CVA process with no money and with HMRC being fully aware of his history and their policy of not signing off on such CVA's, is a mystery. Perhaps he thought his 'tactic' of withholding PAYE and VAT had been a stunning success. Duff and Phelps responded that they had given Whyte an estimate for a quick administration "but, as everyone knows, matters did not work out as he had intended." How very true.

It's not clear why Whyte thought a quick administration in February 2012 was an option. If there was a time to put Rangers into administration and get them back out quickly, it would have been in the summer of 2011, if at all. There seemed little sense in racking up £9m in debt to HMRC and then expecting them to be agreeable in any creditor negotiation. Whyte knew HMRC and knew that HMRC knew him. He was only provoking HMRC the longer he went without paying them.

The largest shareholder of Charles Green's consortium was revealed to be Arif Naqvi, chief executive of a private equity firm called Abraaj Capital, who had acquired 4m of the 25m through a company called Blue Pitch Holdings. Second in line was Margarita Funds Holding Trust whose identity was unknown. Zeus Capital owned shares as did Imran Ahmad (2.2m) and Ally McCoist (1m). Within 24 hours, Green had backtracked on the naming of Blue Pitch Holdings and, on a statement on the Rangers website, said "I would like to clarify that in the case of Blue Pitch Holdings, the legal beneficiary is Mazen Houssami and not Arif Naqvi of Abraaj Capital." Houssami was believed to be a lawyer in the Middle East.

On November 11, Walter Smith returned to Rangers as a non-executive director. He was joined by businessman Ian Hart. Smith saw the role as bringing his experience of Rangers and Scottish football back into the club. He did not foresee an executive role or having any involvement in the running of the football team.

On November 20, the decision of the First Tier Tax Tribunal was published. The Tribunal ruled that most of the payments were loans and not earnings. The tax claim from HMRC would have to be "substantially" reduced. Neil Patey, a partner with Ernst & Young, and regular commentator on football finances, said "Rangers put in place a scheme which was found in the vast majority of cases to be effective, as EBTs have for other companies. There was nothing wrong with EBTs, it was how they were applied and if you stuck within the rules, they were effective. On the basis of the judgment, Rangers stuck within the rules in the vast majority of cases. In a handful they got it wrong."

The majority view of the judges was that "the controversial monies received by the employees were not paid to them as their absolute entitlement. The payments are loans, not earnings, and so are recoverable from the employee or his estate." HMRC said it would consider an appeal.

The news was a humbling one for many across Scottish society. Too many had carried preconceived notions and their own bias into the affair. A blog called the Rangers Tax Case had been in operation since early 2011. Initially, it had been a reasonable source of information, not much of which was in the public domain. It had gradually shifted tone and fallen further behind the curve of the story. The main parties to the FTT decision had received notice of the verdict on October 29 but this had not been leaked on the blog. It had pulled its own plug months earlier and reappeared when it thought the Murray Group, and Rangers, had lost the FTT. Embarrassingly, the blogger had misunderstood the document and, with the heroism one associates with George Orwell, pulled everything again. He (or she) popped back up to say that it had been "accurate on all of the major points of the case except the one that matters most to date -- the outcome". The blogger also expressed the wish that "hopefully, we will see the result reversed on appeal." It had moved from genuine whistleblowing, if it could even be called that, into plain vindictiveness.

The fury of the tax case blog also highlighted the curious morality that many had attached to a matter that didn't belong there in the first place. There had never been any morality or criminality involved. Tax avoidance is a legitimate practice for both individuals and corporations. It has always existed and continues to this day. Even if the Tribunal had gone against Rangers, no crime would have been committed. It was a tax avoidance scheme, not evasion. HMRC thought Rangers owed a certain amount and Rangers thought they owed a different amount. The Tribunal said it was significantly closer to Rangers' version than HMRC's. And that's all it ever was and ever will be. It should not have exercised and outraged as many people as it had done. Jolyon Maugham QC, a tax expert who has commented on the Rangers case said, in his view, "it is not illegal or unlawful to transact to try and attract liability x but to fail and, nevertheless, to attract liability y...that does not establish, on its own, that we have behaved unlawfully or illegally. It is not unlawful or illegal to make an honest mistake."

Seeking to minimise tax has been carried out on a personal and corporate level across the country, and in Scottish football, for many years. In recent years, a number of players, from different clubs, have declared personal bankruptcy to avoid any liability from an involvement in a failed tax avoidance scheme. It happens and the Rangers situation did not deserve the mass hysteria that it received. The EBT scheme at Rangers was always complex. It had never been a black and white issue and yet many had come to view it as such with an almost zealot-like belief in its representation of good versus evil.

It was a bittersweet victory. The club had been vindicated to some extent but was now left dealing with the fallout. Had the use of the EBT scheme by the Murray Group been worth it? Clearly not. There was no evidence that any sporting advantage had been achieved. The peak year for EBT contributions at Rangers was 2006 when £9m was paid into the trusts. This was a year when Rangers finished outside the top two for the first time in 18 years and saw the end of Alex McLeish's time as manager. If there was a correlation between EBT use and on-field success, it was not an obvious one. Nor was there any evidence that any player had been enticed to Ibrox solely on the promise of access to the Employee Benefit Trust scheme. The curious argument that Rangers had signed players they could not afford didn't stack up either. Rangers did pay £47m into the trusts over the years. If the club had paid this as income instead, and then paid income tax as the club had always done, then any additional debt accrued would have been absorbed into bank borrowings or inter-group lending as was common at that time.

Any advantage, if it even existed, was completely dwarfed by the consequence of HMRC's decision to pursue Rangers over the matter. It had spooked Lloyds. Rangers' debts had fallen from £35m to £17m in four years but the possibility of a victory by HMRC had left it difficult for the club to function. It had led directly to the Craig Whyte takeover, the unnecessary administration of the club and now the club plying its trade in the Scottish Third Division. The club had gone through an administration it didn't need to go through and then had a CVA rejected by HMRC on the basis of a claim that the First Tier Tax Tribunal had now ruled was largely invalid. From Rangers' point of view, the entire scheme had been an unnecessary risk by David Murray. The FTT verdict camouflaged the fact that Murray had taken over one of the biggest clubs in the UK in 1988 and had left with a pound in his pocket and the club picking up the pieces from his decision making.

In December, Charles Green launched the Rangers International Football Club plc onto the Alternative Investment Market. It raised £22m - £17m from institutional investors and £5.2m from supporters. Green was listed as the largest shareholder at 14.9% with the expectation that this would be diluted. Other shareholders were Blue Pitch, Margarita, Mike

Ashley, Imran Ahmad, Richard Hughes of Zeus Capital, Ally McCoist, Craig Mather and Norne Anstalt. New Institutional Investors included Legal & General Investment Management, Artemis Investment Management LLP, Hargreave Hale Limited and Insight Investment Management (Global) Limited.

Almost as soon as the floatation was over, and at the prompting of Charles Green, the board had asked chairman Malcolm Murray to stand down. Murray had been useful in the IPO as his background in fund management meant he had many contacts in the City as well as bringing credibility to the table. Perhaps more than other people involved at the time. He had set up meetings with potential investors and institutions. Perhaps he had now outlived his usefulness.

The last of the football debts inherited by Charles Green were settled in February although perhaps in a more opportunistic way than one would have liked. Rapid Vienna had been owed £975,000 from the transfer of Nikica Jelavic but settled for £715,000. Hearts had been owed a final payment of £500,000 for Lee Wallace. Green had tried to exploit Hearts' own financial woes in November by offering them a reduced amount to settle. They refused then but settled for £400,000 in February. Other reduced fees were agreed for Mervan Celik, Alejandro Bedoya and Dorin Goian.

On February 28, the SPL independent commission, chaired by Lord Nimmo Smith, published their findings into the 'undisclosed payments' issue. They ruled that Rangers had not gained any "unfair competitive advantage" but the club had failed to disclose 'side letters' detailing payments to players on the EBT scheme. Rangers would be fined £250,000 for breaches of disclosure rules but no further punishment.

The commission wrote that "Rangers FC did not gain any unfair competitive advantage from the contraventions of the SPL Rules in failing to make proper disclosure of the side-letter arrangements, nor did the non-disclosure have the effect that any of the registered players were ineligible to play and, for this and other reasons, no sporting sanction or penalty should be imposed upon Rangers FC."

The crucial element to the conclusion was that any failure to disclose 'side letters' was not done in order to gain an advantage on the field. The players were correctly registered with the SPL and SFA. The 'side letters' were not disclosed in order to maximise the benefits of the EBT scheme. The SFA's head of registrations, Sandy Bryson, had given evidence to the commission to the effect that any player, once registered with the SFA, remained registered until that registration was revoked. Any undisclosed payments to a player did not render the registration as invalid. It was not possible to retrospectively terminate the registration of a player. All Rangers' players registrations were valid.

Nor did the commission conclude that any disclosure would have had any impact on HMRC's treatment of EBT's, in any case. "Moreover, we have received no evidence from which we could possibly say that oldco could not or would not have entered into the EBT arrangements with players if it had been required to comply with the requirement to disclose the arrangements. It is entirely possible that the EBT arrangements could have been disclosed to the SPL and SFA without prejudicing the argument - accepted by the majority of the [First Tier] Tax Tribunal - that such arrangements, resulting in loans made to the players, did not give rise to payments absolutely or unreservedly held for or to the order of the individual players."

It had been a mistake, though understandable, for Green to refuse to co-operate with the SPL commission. After the attempted blackmail of Rangers in the summer, it was not unreasonable to think that the commission was working backwards from the verdict. He was, however, triumphant after the verdict and requested that certain SPL chairmen should apologise to the Rangers support. This did not happen. Instead, the SPL asked Rangers to pay £500,000 legal costs for setting up the commission.

The half-yearly results came out at the end of March. The club had lost £7m up to December 2012 but had cash in the bank of £21.2m. The player wage bill had fallen from £27m to £7m – a stark illustration of where the club was now at. A total of 38,000 season tickets had been sold for the Scottish Third Division.

Whyte resurfaced at the beginning of April to claim ownership of Rangers and that Charles Green had been his front man. Green had used Sevco 5088 to purchase Whyte's shares. When the CVA failed, Green transferred the assets to another off-the-shelf company called Sevco Scotland. Sevco Scotland had since been renamed Rangers Football Club Ltd and then floated as Rangers International Football Club plc (or RIFC plc) on the Alternative Investment Market.

Whyte claimed Imran Ahmad had introduced Charles Green and a businessman called Rafat Rizvi to him in London in May 2012. Whyte alleged that he and Aidan Earley would have a majority shareholding in Sevco 5088 and Ahmad, Rizvi, Green and Earley would share £250,000 and 10% of share capital raised. Whyte recorded their conversations. In one of his recordings, Green can be heard saying to him "you are Sevco, that's what we are saying." Green responded that he was only trying to keep Whyte sweet in order to get his shares from him to do the CVA. He called Whyte "delusional" and that he and Ahmad had simply told Whyte "whatever he wanted to hear." As the CVA failed, Green said that Whyte's shares were no longer needed and the deal was off.

He had registered 'Sevco Scotland' at the end of May.

Whyte was suing for £50m claiming he'd been "swindled". Whyte had paid Ahmad £137,500. It was sitting in Ahmad's mum's account. Trying to return it, Whyte refused to accept it. A Rangers spokesman said, "He has threatened to take Duff & Phelps to court, the SFA to court and now Charles Green and Imran Ahmad. We suggest he gets on with it. We would be delighted to see him there." The spokesman said Ahmad had paid the £200,000 exclusivity fee to Duff and Phelps himself and that "the £137,500 dropped into the account of Mr Ahmad's mother because no one involved in the takeover wanted any of the disgraced former owner's money to go near the business account. Attempts have been made to return this money but Mr Whyte refuses to accept it back and records will show it has never been touched or used."

Enter Worthington Group. Worthington purchased 26% of Law Financial Ltd, a company owned by Craig Whyte and which had Sevco 5088 as one of its subsidiaries. Law Financial was instigating the legal action on behalf of Whyte against Charles Green. Duff and Phelps had been clear that Sevco Scotland had purchased the assets and that Whyte's claim had no basis. Worthington, however, were a curious oddity in their own right. Over the next few years, they would report Charles Green to the Serious Fraud Office and have their shares suspended, twice, at their own request. In October 2014, The Times reported that Worthington's largest stakeholder was a company called Regenesis. The major shareholder of Regenesis was Wulsten Earley, brother of Aidan Earley, an associate of Whyte, and fellow director of Sevco 5088, who had received £250,000, via Rangers, to Banstead Athletic, Earley's football club. The Financial Times would describe Worthington as a company that seemed to exist solely to print shares. The company was liquidated in 2017.

Whilst threatening everyone else with court action, Whyte found himself once again on the losing end at the High Court in London in May. A judge ruled that Whyte had lied to Ticketus during his takeover of Rangers. He was ordered to pay £700,000 in legal costs and interest and was now on the hook for £20m in the 'personal and corporate guarantees' that he'd given to Ticketus.

Whyte had been sent a questionnaire by Ticketus as part of his loan application to borrow against Rangers' season ticket money. The questionnaire asked if he had "at any time been accused of any fraud, deception, misfeasance, breach of trust or other misconduct?" Whyte replied that he hadn't. It then asked if he'd been "disqualified from working as a director (or being involved in the management) of a company?" Whyte again replied that he hadn't. Both of these were not true. At the Chancery Division of the High Court in London, Master Matthew Marsh said that "The inescapable conclusion on the evidence is that Mr Whyte knew his answers were false. Even if I am wrong about that, he was reckless on whether the answers were accurate, and provided them not caring whether they were true. Alternatively he was negligent in failing to check the accuracy of the questionnaire before passing it on."

On the back of Whyte's claims, the Rangers board launched an independent investigation, to be conducted by Deloitte and Pinsent Masons, into Green's alleged links with Craig Whyte. "The independent report will be commissioned and completed as speedily as possible and presented directly to the non-executive directors of the company. The chief executive will not be involved in the conduct of the examination." On May 19, Charles Green resigned as chief executive. Green cited the "negative publicity" as a factor and denied any "wrong-doing". Craig Mather would replace him as chief executive.

Green agreed to sell his shares to James and Sandy Easdale. The pair already owned 6% and the acquisition of Green's shareholding would take them to 14%. Green had bought five million shares in Rangers at 1p each in October 2012. As of May 2013, they stood at 57.5p each, making them worth £2.9m. It would be a £2.4m profit for less than a year's work. The shares could not be sold until December as per Stock Market rules.

Green's resignation was quickly followed by that of Imran Ahmad as commercial director. Ahmad had been accused of posting messages on a supporters messageboard that were critical of Walter Smith and Ally McCoist.

Over the year, Charles Green had been paid £933,000 which included a severance payment of £217,850. Imran Ahmad was on a £350,000 salary plus expenses with an unspecified bonus. He received a £50,000 payment for giving Rangers a short-term loan of £200,000 to pay Duff and Phelps the exclusivity fee. Only £178,000 of that was repaid with the remainder converted into shares. When Rangers floated, Ahmad had 2.2 million shares. Costing him around £22,000, Ahmad sold the shares in August for £830,000. Nice work if you can get it.

SIX

May 2013 - May 2014

Any hope that the support had that the club might normalise after the departure of Whyte was already wafer thin. It would only deteriorate over the next 18 months as in-fighting, boardroom reshuffling and jostling for power became an almost weekly occurrence.

Chairman Malcolm Murray had refused to stand down and a smear campaign was started against him. He was accused of being indiscreet about club business and that other members of the board, and supporters, had issues with his conduct. A vote of no confidence was followed by a legal letter served on the club on behalf of the mysterious Blue Pitch Holdings calling for Murray's resignation and that of non-executive director, Phil Cartmell. The club had 21 days to make the changes or face an EGM. Blue Pitch had teamed up with James and Sandy Easdale and this bloc amounted to 29% of the club. They also wanted Chris Morgan of Blue Pitch Holdings and James Easdale to given seats on the board.

A video was leaked of Malcolm Murray drunk in a restaurant in London some months earlier. The video had been uploaded to YouTube but had been filmed by finance director, Brian Stockbridge. Murray claimed to have a medical condition and that he'd been plied with drink at the meal. Whatever the truth of the matter, it had been classless to film and even lower for the material to then appear in public. Stockbridge claimed it had never been the intention for it be in available in public. Perhaps only for his own personal gratification. In the end, Malcolm Murray resigned as chairman and was replaced by Walter Smith. On July 9, Malcolm Murray left the club and James Easdale was confirmed as a director.

Murray then teamed up with Paul Murray (no relation) and another shareholder, Frank Blin, to submit a requisition for an EGM where resolutions would be put forward to remove Craig Mather, Brian Stockbridge and Bryan Smart as directors and appoint Malcolm Murray, Paul Murray and Frank Blin as directors.

In the space of a year, Walter Smith had gone from leading a consortium to non-executive director and now chairman. Smith was essentially a good man who just wanted Rangers to do well. The best intentions were not enough, however. On August 5, after just over two months, he resigned as chairman. Smith had enjoyed a stable board in both his times as manager and, perhaps, saw the opportunity in accepting Charles Green's invitation, to help his chosen successor, Ally McCoist, have the same stability. It was not to be. Smith called the board "dysfunctional" and that the board could "rarely find consensus and agreement". It was an impossible situation. He backed the proposed motions in the Murray EGM but offered his support to new chief executive, Craig Mather, who, he said, was doing a "good job".

In May, the Insolvency Practitioners Association, had cleared Duff and Phelps of misconduct and a conflict of interest in their involvement with the club. The Association agreed with Duff and Phelps that their original discussion with Whyte had only been an estimate. In its letter, the IPA said the original quotation was provided on a different basis to the actual work carried out.

The report by law firm Pinsent Masons, forensic investigators Deloitte and Roy Martin QC, into the alleged links between Charles Green and Craig Whyte found no evidence that Whyte's claims had any substance. Both Whyte and Aidan Earley had been asked for their evidence but had refused. In a statement to the London Stock Exchange, Rangers said "The investigation found no evidence that Craig Whyte had any involvement with Sevco Scotland Limited (now called The Rangers Football Club Limited), the company which ultimately acquired the business and assets of The Rangers Football Club PLC from its administrators; nor which would suggest that Craig Whyte invested in The Rangers Football Club Limited or Rangers International Football Club plc."

Charles Green agreed to sell 714,825 of his 5m shares to Laxey Partners, an Isle of Man-based hedge fund. The deal could not be completed until December. In August, he returned to Ibrox on a 'consultancy' basis on a contract of £1,000 a month. His remit was, seemingly, to promote Rangers' interests and work on shareholder relations. Green immediately got to work on shareholder relations by offering to sell his shares to potential buyers for £14m. It was a bargain no one was willing to take up.

On August 20, Charles Green resigned for a second time, this time from his invaluable role as a consultant, a position he'd managed to hold for 18 days. Sandy Easdale claimed to have agreed with Green to purchase the remainder of his shares when the lock-in period ended in December 2013. Sandy joined his brother on the board in September. His personal shareholding had increased to 4.37% and the club announced to the Stock Exchange that Easdale now had voting rights of 23.8%, believed to be the proxies of Blue Pitch Holdings and Margarita Holdings.

In an agreement with the club, the requisitioners EGM request was to be carried out at the AGM. The condition was that AGM had to take place by October. The club had said it would cost £150,000 to have separate meetings. The requisitioners withdrew their motion.

In August, Dave King predicted further financial mayhem ahead. The £22m raised in the IPO had largely gone, he said, and whilst the club had received a short-term financial boost through season tickets, King believed the board would eventually run out of road.

The situation was even worse than King imagined. At a meeting with supporters' groups on August 8, Brian Stockbridge admitted the £22m had gone completely in the space of eight months. Chief executive Craig Mather, Ally McCoist and new director of communications James Traynor were also at the meeting. Stockbridge had received a 100% bonus for Rangers winning the Scottish Third Division – another £200,000 on top of his £200,000 salary. Stockbridge told supporters that £3m had gone on legal and stockbroker fees.

Imran Ahmad launched a £3.4m legal battle against the club. He said he would settle outside of court for £500,000 plus legal costs. He claimed to have a letter from Charles Green promising him a £500,000 bonus for working for the club for 12 months. He also believed he was due 5% of all commercial deals negotiated by him and had been awarded 2m shares at 1p each. At a preliminary hearing, Alan Summers QC, for Rangers, said Ahmad's argument was "breathtaking in its audacity." Ahmad's claim did not hinge on a contractual entitlement but on an "independent, unilateral exercise of power by a CEO" to hand over

£500,000. The court needed to establish, he said, whether Charles Green had the authority to issue such a letter and how Rangers could be bound by the terms of such a letter. Lord Woolman agreed and the case was held over until December.

The annual accounts to June 2013 recorded a £14.3m operating loss. There had been a post-tax profit of £1.2m. On revenues of £19.1m, the club was spending £7.8m on player wages. The ratio was 43%. It also recorded that Charles Green's bonus of £360,000 was greater than his salary of £333,077. Deloittes had been paid nearly £600,000.

Craig Mather and Brian Stockbridge flew to South Africa to meet Dave King in September. King had paid the South African authorities £44m the previous month to settle his dispute with them. King's preference was to invest in the club, through a new share issue, rather than buy existing shares. Mather and Stockbridge had offered him the possibility of becoming chairman.

A new motion submitted by Paul Murray and Jim McColl which called for the appointment of Murray, Malcolm Murray, Scott Murdoch and Alex Wilson to the board was blocked by the board. In response, Murray and McColl went to the Court of Session to secure an interim interdict preventing October's AGM from going ahead. Paul Murray repeated his call for Mather and Stockbridge to go.

Mather duly obliged, resigning on October 16. Ian Hart and Bryan Smart also resigned as non-executive directors. The AGM would now take place on December 19. Two new appointments were made. David Somers was appointed chairman and Graham Wallace was appointed chief executive. Wallace's background at Manchester City certainly suggested a level of professionalism that perhaps had not been there.

Laxey Partners became the largest shareholder in mid-November when it purchased an additional 3.3m shares, taking its stake to 11.64%. Laxey had already agreed to purchase 700,000 of Charles Green's shares in December. At their request, Norman Crighton was added as a non-executive director. Laxey had been wavering on the issue of boardroom change and had indicated they would support the moves of Paul Murray and Jim McColl. They now announced they would back the board in the upcoming AGM with the rationale that the appointments of Somers, Wallace and Crighton and the departures of Green, Mather and Ahmad were the necessary refresh that the club needed.

At the end of November, Craig Whyte was making his familiar journey to the courtrooms. He was appealing against the Ticketus decision from earlier in the year. He asked Deputy High judge David Halpern QC to overturn the ruling. Whyte claimed that the document submitted to Ticketus, containing false information over his past disqualifications, had been "prepared by his solicitors" and that he'd expected them to check.

His argument was rejected by the judge who compared Whyte to the Dickens character Wilkins Micawber, from the novel David Copperfield, noted for his unjustified optimism. The judge said that "it was argued that the case should go to trial because of its complexity and financial value and because Mr Whyte is disadvantaged in not having the relevant documents or legal resources. In my judgment the Master was right to reject these arguments, which I regard as pure Micawberism.'

Whyte had also made an appearance at Inverness Sheriff Court where he'd been required to read out a letter allegedly written by his former housekeeper, whom he'd now accused of stealing from him. Jane Hagan and Terence Horan, his former caretaker, were accused of stealing valuables from Whyte's former home in Grantown-on-Spey. Hagan had written a note to a friend where she said Whyte "has been behaving rather badly" and "his living is mostly by dubious means" and that "he is not a good man." The couple claimed they hadn't been paid by Whyte and the court had also heard of non-payment of tax and national insurance, which sounds familiar, as well as the couple dealing with phone calls from the bank over non-payment of the mortgage. The couple were fined £1000 each by the sheriff who expressed some sympathy for them. The castle was repossessed by the bank.

The good news continued for him. Liberty Capital, the company Whyte had used to buy Rangers and which, Whyte had claimed, had investments across all business sectors, went into liquidation over an unpaid legal bill of £5000.

In the run-up to the AGM, Sandy Easdale had a further 3.1% of voting rights assigned to him by Beaufort Securities. Easdale now held voting rights over a total of 26.6%. But Ally McCoist handed the voting rights to his one million shares to his local supporters club, the Calderwood Loyal RSC in East Kilbride. It was expected that they would vote against the board.

The December 2013 AGM was perhaps one of the most ramshackle and angry in Rangers' history. The Rangers board walked out to a wall of jeering and booing from the approximately 1,600 shareholders present in the Main Stand. Graham Wallace said he was now starting a "120-day business review" to look at all the costs. Brian Stockbridge said that £6.5m had went on costs of the IPO. This was broken down as commission of £2m, legal fees of £1.6m, valuation fees of £1.5m, printing costs of £328,000, PR costs of £100,000 and, best of all, financial advisory costs at £2.5m. The last number provoked outrage from the audience. It had all sounded like something from Yes, Minister.

The attempt by the requisitioners to get on the board failed with Malcolm Murray securing 29.8%,

Paul Murray (31.7%), Scott Murdoch (30%) and Alex Wilson (29.9%). It had not been enough. But, before the AGM, the ever-prescient Dave King had made it clear he was happy to play the long game and predicted that, in two years, the shareholder profile would look very different.

Brian Stockbridge managed only 65.3% of the vote. He left the club a month later. Under pressure from Laxey Partners, he had repaid his bonus for winning the Scottish Third Division. Wallace brought in former Arsenal and Liverpool finance director Philip Nash as a consultant.

Graham Wallace had assured the AGM that funds were in place to get to the end of the season. Yet within weeks of the AGM, Ally McCoist was asked by Wallace if he would go to the players and ask that they take a 15% pay cut. There was no mention that any of the board or executive team would do likewise. The players, understandably, refused.

There was a lot of ill-informed comment around this time that the wages being paid to the players was too much and that it was a big factor in the financial mismanagement of the club rather than decisions taken at executive level now or in the past. It was very easy to look at someone like Ian Black, reportedly on £6,000 a week, and consider him an extravagant waste of money. The players may not always perform but player wages to turnover was around 43%. This was not an unhealthy figure.

At the end of February, it was announced that Rangers had borrowed £1.5m from Sandy Easdale and Laxey Partners, less than two months after Wallace had told the AGM that no additional funding would be required. Easdale was lending the club £500,000 on a no fee, no interest basis. Laxey Partners were lending the club £1m. Both loans had to be repaid by September 1 with Laxey Partners being paid an additional £150,000 interest on repayment. Moreover, the loans were secured against the Albion car park and Edmiston House.

A wealthy supporter, George Letham, went public that he would replace the Laxey loan on the same terms but with interest reduced from £150,000 to £75,000. The security on the loan would be canceled and the £75,000 would be converted by Letham into shares. Laxey agreed to the transfer and the club took Letham's loan.

Dave King proposed that fans pay their season ticket money into a trust and the money would be released to the club on a 'pay-as-they-play' basis or season ticket money is placed into a trust and released in full to the club against security of club property until all games are played. King had the support of an umbrella group called The Union of Fans.

It was clear that supporter numbers were down from the initial optimism of the 2012-13 season and that supporters were becoming fatigued and disenchanted. There appeared to be no good news on the horizon and the club had seemingly gone from the frying pan of the Whyte era into a fire.

King appeared to be the only person with a vision on how Rangers could go forward. Identifying that the team and the club needed massive investment (correctly calling, a year early, that the team might not even win the Championship), he called for a fresh share issue to allow investors, like him, to invest directly into the club. The club needed soft investment to get anywhere near its previous income base. Costs had to drive revenue, he said. Scrambling around for £1.5m loans in February and asking players to pay cuts in January was only going to be a downward spiral.

On April 25, Graham Wallace revealed the outcome of his 120-day business review. It made for grim reading. By his own admission, Wallace considered the situation "worse than I expected". The club had gone through almost £70m in nearly two years. £700,000 was spent on lawyers' fees whilst, perversely, the review admitted that deals had been signed on behalf of the club without any lawyers being present. It referred to "onerous contracts" that were not delivering "value on price or service". The board in 2012 had made "flawed" assumptions on the amount and timing of income from Rangers Retail. £8.6m was attributed to "central administration and overheads." £2m was spent on WiFi at the stadium, LED displays and "jumbo screens." Bizarrely, £5.5m from Charles Green's purchase of the club was also included. Had Rangers' own money, as in the Whyte takeover, been used to purchase Rangers? Wallace said he did not have an answer for that.

£3m had been spent on football debts and £2.6m on purchasing the Albion car park and Edmiston House. Of the £70.7m raised in ticket sales, commercial revenues and share issue proceeds between May 2012 and December 2013, only £3.5m was left by December 2013. When the club needed to rebuild, the scouting and recruitment network was "dismantled." Six figures were being spent on public relations whilst the club did not have a single scout for the football team. It was a car crash.

SEVEN

May 2014 - March 2015

Season 2013-14 had ended with the support and the board in open warfare. Dave King's plan for a separate fund for season ticket money might have fallen through but there was clearly significant wariness amongst the support. By the end of May, with the renewal date passed, the club had sold only around 14,000 season tickets. Moreover, in the terms of the loans taken from Sandy Easdale and George Letham in February, the £1.5m had to be repaid as soon as the club had funds to do so. Neither loan had been repaid.

Most supporters would pay for season tickets by instalments. The ability to pay by credit card was unavailable after the company providing the service, First Data, had withdrawn the facility. First Data had sought security before providing their services which Graham Wallace had blamed on supporters boycotting. It then transpired First Data had indicated their need for security in January although supporters were not told that credit card payments would not be accepted until April.

The Upper Tier Tax Tribunal recorded its verdict in July in HMRC's appeal after the First Tier Tax Tribunal. It was another defeat for HMRC. Lord Doherty agreed with the FTT. This time David Murray came out swinging and blamed HMRC for the long-running saga. He said that it had put off buyers and stated that if Craig Whyte had "fulfilled his contractual obligations and responsibilities" the club "would not have gone into administration or liquidation." Murray said he'd always been confident in the case.

Murray's anger was misplaced. He had left Rangers to play Russian roulette with a bullet he'd loaded in the gun. If he was confident there was no bullet in the barrel, he should have pulled the trigger himself. Instead, he left Rangers dealing with the problem he'd created and then, three years later, claiming he knew it wouldn't come to anything. It simply didn't wash.

It was unfortunate, too, that some rallied to Murray's defence after the UTT verdict. Ally McCoist suggested that Murray was owed an apology. From whom, it wasn't clear. One understands, and perhaps even admires, a certain loyalty but Murray had long crossed the Rubicon at Rangers.

Two tax tribunals, adjudicated by tax experts, had now found against HMRC. But this wouldn't be the end of the matter. HMRC would go again and this time to the law courts.

In August, the Daily Record ran with the unsurprising news that HMRC were already in pursuit of Craig Whyte when he took over Rangers in May 2011. Having bolted from the UK in 1999, HMRC discovered in 2010 that Whyte had been living in the UK since 2005. He had consistently refused to submit proper tax returns leading HMRC to calculate demands of £1m for 2006-07 and £1.2m for 2007-08. For 2006-07, Whyte had claimed he only had £24 in bank interest as income. Yet he would tell Ticketus that he was worth £33m and this constituted his personal guarantee to them. In a working example of being hoisted by your own petard, it was this guarantee, which ended up in the hands of HMRC, that allowed them to present Whyte with a bill for £3,741,835.29. Only right for a man of such independent means.

In August, too, Rangers would propose a new share issue of £4m. The initial plan was to try and raise £8m. Again, it appeared like the club was living on a month-to-month basis with no plan on how to develop or change the situation. On the eve of the new season, around 21,000 season tickets had been sold – down 15,000 on the previous year's total.

Graham Wallace's 120-day business review in April had referred to 'onerous contracts' and deals being signed without lawyers present. In September, one such contract became public. It emerged that, in 2012, Charles Green had sold the naming rights to Ibrox to Mike Ashley for £1. The contract had only become public due to an answer given to a newspaper by Sandy Easdale. It was claimed that Green then spent £250,000 of the club's money on legal fees to try and get the contract cancelled. Charles Green appeared to be a lot of things but he did not appear to be stupid.

Ashley had the power to rename Ibrox at any time. There was no appetite in the Rangers support for the stadium to be renamed, in any case. The fact it had been handed over for £1 was doubly sickening. Earlier in the year, Scottish Rugby had secured £20m from BT for the renaming of Murrayfield. Whatever the Ibrox naming deal was, it was certainly not one that had any commercial logic.

Ashley's influence at the club was starting to grow. A day later, the club announced that the main retail superstore at Ibrox and Rangers stores in Belfast and Glasgow Airport had been transferred to Sports Direct. Fifty-one staff would be transferred under TUPE to Sports Direct.

Imran Ahmad's court case against the club continued in September where he was able to have £620,000 frozen from the club's bank account. At the Court of Session, it was claimed the club only had £1.2m in the bank. And now £620,000 was unavailable. Ahmad was claiming for £500,000 plus £120,000 in legal costs. Prior to the hearing, Sandy Easdale had told the press that Rangers' finances were "fragile". It was a kind of foot-in-mouth that earned him a scathing attack from the Union of Fans who noted that it was not the first time Easdale had made damaging comments about the club's finances in public. And doing so before a hearing when the club was arguing the opposite was baffling, to say the least. Three years after the club had suffered the indignity of such court cases under Whyte's regime, it seemed to be a nasty case of déjà vu and the club being no further forward.

Ahmad's case was settled out of court. The club would not say the amount other than to say it was "significantly less" than the £620,000 that had been ring-fenced by the court. Ahmad's legal costs would have been fixed at £120,000 so the club would still be paying anything from £300,000 to £400,000.

The share issue, therefore, brought in a much needed £3.1m. Nineteen million shares had been made available at 20p each. Five million were purchased by Laxey Partners, taking its stake to 16.3%. Mike Ashley had told the Stock Exchange he would not be taking part in the offer. It was sticking plaster stuff. The initial idea of raising £8m had been reduced to a target of £4m. Now the offer had fallen £900,000 short of even that target. It was not a long-term solution.

Seeking an emergency loan, Graham Wallace had spoken to Mike Ashley. Ashley demanded ownership of the Rangers badge in return for the loan. Wallace refused. This was why Ashley did not participate in the open offer – where money would have gone to the club – but instead purchased the 4.2m shares of Hargreave Hale for £840,000. Ashley now had an 8.9% stake, second only to Laxey Partners.

In October, Craig Whyte was banned from being a company director in the UK for 15 years. The Insolvency Service said Whyte had acted "deliberately and dishonestly" in how he'd funded the takeover of Rangers. The acquisition, they said, "was entirely predicated upon an untruth and the untruth was he would be funding the acquisition with his own personal wealth or that of his company." Rangers had effectively been used to purchase their own shares. Whyte had run Rangers "without reference to other board directors, preventing RFC from being subject to proper corporate governance."

Lord Tyre at the Court of Session was less kind. He said there was a "strongly arguable case" that Whyte had committed a criminal offence by using Ticketus as it had amounted to "financial assistance, prohibited by Section 678 of the Companies Act 2006, and accordingly constituted an offence". Whyte's conduct was a "combination of dishonesty, disregard for the interests of the companies to which he owed duties and the creditors of those companies, use of Crown debts to finance trade, misappropriation of company funds (at least in the case of Tixway) for private purposes and wilful breach of a director's administrative duties". Whyte had "demonstrated a reckless disregard for the interests of the company to which he owed fiduciary duties."

Whyte was not present at the hearing. Officials from the Department of Business Innovation and Skills could not trace him to tell him of the date of the hearing. He'd also failed to attend hearings into his Ticketus case. At the High Court, Mr Justice Arnold noted that Whyte "has adopted a policy of evading service and failing to communicate with the claimants' solicitors, and in those ways he seeks to frustrate the court's orders."

Graham Wallace and Philip Nash met with Paul Murray, Dave King and George Letham at the start of October to discuss the possibility of a cash injection. King's offer was for £16m for 51% of RIFC plc but would also require a new share issue and would need to be approved by at least 75% of votes at the AGM. Mike Ashley reacted to the news by requesting an EGM to vote on the removal of Graham Wallace and Philip Nash from the board.

Philip Nash resigned the day before the club accepted a £2m loan from Mike Ashley on October 25. Nash and Wallace had opposed the loan. King's offer relied on 75% shareholder approval and with Ashley at 8.9%, Laxey Partners, the Easdale and their proxies, they could easily get over 50% to oppose. Brian Kennedy, a one-time bidder for the club, had also offered emergency funding of £3m with the condition of one seat on the board. Ashley wanted two seats on the board plus security over the Albion car park and Edmiston House for his £2m. Nash resigned believing the offer not to be in the club's interests. Graham Wallace would soon follow. Wallace had been outvoted on the board by James Easdale, David Somers and Norman Crighton. Derek Llambias and Sports Direct executive Barry Leach were given consultant roles at the club.

On November 14, Gary Withey, David Grier, Paul Clark and David Whitehouse were arrested in a joint operation involving Surrey Police, Cheshire Police and Thames Valley Police. A warrant was issued for Craig Whyte's arrest. All four were to appear at Glasgow Sheriff Court facing charges relating to the "alleged fraudulent acquisition" of the club. The charges alleged Whyte duped three companies including Ticketus into handing him more than £22million.

A second arrest warrant was issued for Whyte after he, again, failed to attend a court hearing in London over his failure to repay Ticketus the money they had been awarded in April 2013. Whyte was arrested in Mexico City, stopping over on a flight from Japan before trying to get to Costa Rica.

The accounts to June 30, 2014 recorded an £8.3m loss, down from £14m the previous year. Staff costs had fallen £3m and season ticket revenue had dropped. The ratio of wages from players to turnover was now at 26%. The full extent of the 'onerous contracts' was becoming apparent. Fans had spent £7.6m on retail but the club had earned only £590,000 from Rangers Retail – half of which was owned by Mike Ashley. In fact, it's not even clear that Rangers received that money. Rangers Retail also had a contractual obligation to purchase stock at a higher price than it could sell it. he club had gone from a minimum of £4.8m a year from JJB Sports to, potentially, only £2,000. Supporters groups called for a boycott of club's stores and Sports Direct.

In many respects, the autumn of 2014 felt much darker, more serious for Rangers than the events of 2012 did. In 2012, there had been an inevitable sense of defiance and perhaps some naïve optimism. Once the season was under way, there were full houses, tweets of #thejourney, talk of going through the divisions unbeaten, perhaps even winning one of the cups whilst in the lower leagues. The response of the support and the December 2012 share issue gave the belief that the club could regroup and rebound quicker than expected.

On the field, by autumn 2014, the journey through the leagues had become a slog. Two years of playing part-time opposition had taken its toll on the standards of the team. Even so, it also seemed that the team was not as up to speed in performance, preparation and professionalism as perhaps it should have been. It was looking unlikely that the team could actually win the Championship so would have to achieve promotion through the play-offs, if possible.

There was no £20m share issue appearing over the horizon this time. The club had signed 'onerous contracts', said Graham Wallace, and the details of merchandising and retail contracts, naming rights going for a pound whilst the club lived seemingly off emergency loans every couple of months gave a depressing feel to the whole situation. It wasn't clear how the club was going to grow its way out of the situation as it felt like it was being slowly suffocated.

The organized boycotts of the Union of Fans and Sons of Struth had reduced season ticket numbers for 2014-15. In August 2014, for a Petrofac Training Cup game against Clyde, a crowd of 11,190 had turned up – the lowest home attendance in 29 years. The Scottish Cup exit to Raith Rovers was also watched by just 11,422. Halfway through the season, the club was averaging 25,538 a game. The support was at the end of its patience and had had enough.

The AGM had been called for December 22. Eleven days beforehand, Norman Crighton, Laxey Partners man on the board, left the board. It would be a significant move.

Prior to the AGM, the SFA issued notices of complaint against Rangers and Mike Ashley alleging breaches of an undertaking about his influence on the day-to-day running of the club. Two years earlier, Ashley had given an undertaking to the SFA not to own more than 10% of Rangers nor have any influence at the club. Ashley's response to the notice of complaints was to appoint Derek Llambias as chief executive. It was a public two-fingered salute.

The 2014 AGM was even rowdier than the previous year. The board were greeted with a chorus of boos and jeers. The crowd began chanting "out, out, out." The board were unfazed. If anything, David Somers seemed to thrive on the abuse, like some sleazy masochist. "When you get to be chairman of Rangers, you can do it your way" sneered Somers at shareholders. It was an unholy mess. A board that was antagonistic and provoking supporters and supporters that loathed each and every one of them. There seemed to be no way forward.

David Somers received just 61% of the ballot for re-election. It was enough but reflected the widespread distrust of him as chairman. This would only get worse when, just after the AGM, emails from Somers to Mike Ashley's lawyer were leaked online to supporters group Sons of Struth. Somers, who had posed as an impartial chairman doing his best for the club, had pleaded with the Ashley camp to block Dave King's bid in October as it would cost him his place in the board along with that of the Easdales. He wrote, "Meanwhile I have received a formal proposal for a deal from Dave King and my board are clamouring for a board call to discuss it and no doubt approve it. A board on which James and I are in a minority. Dave King's proposal includes board seats, which means Sandy, James and I will not survive on this board very much longer."

Resolution 9 at the AGM had been to "enable the directors' authority for the disapplication of pre-memption rights." It had been proposed by the Easdales and would have allowed the company to have a share issue that would be open to the public. The Easdales then voted against it. The school of thought was that, by rejecting it, the SFA would be forced into a position of allowing Mike Ashley to increase his shareholding and effectively takeover the club.

Derek Llambias was dispatched by Ashley to meet with the SFA to make the case for Ashley to be allowed to increase his stake from 8.9% to 29.9%. This was rejected by the SFA. They had become aware of another party which could provide credible funding to the club. Douglas Park, George Letham and George Taylor - known as the Three Bears - had emailed the club with an offer to purchase all of the 40m shares in resolutions 8 and 9 for £6.5m.

The year ended with a stunning shift in power. First, Laxey Partners sold their 16.3% stake to the Douglas Park, George Letham and George Taylor consortium for £2.6m. Laxey Partners boss Colin

Kingsnorth said: "I sold because a fans-based group were hopefully going to be the best placed to take on Mike Ashley's power. After Ashley removed Norman Crighton, his most vocal critic, it was obvious David Somers was just a wet fish agreeing anything Ashley wanted." The sale had caught Ashley, the Easdales and Somers unaware.

And then Dave King purchased the shares of Artemis and Miton giving him a 14.5% stake. George Taylor had his personal stake so this, combined with the Three Bears and Dave King's stake came to 34.1%. There would be other investors who would support this bloc. There was now a rival power base.

Ashley did not take this gracefully. Despite the presence of other investors, a £10m loan was arranged by the board with Ashley's Sports Direct. The terms of the proposal were onerous. Ashley would have security over Ibrox Stadium and the Auchenhowie training ground. The previous April the board had issued a statement stating they had "no intention of granting security over Ibrox to anybody." This was followed up with another statement in the summer promising not to use the stadium in any form of "sale, securitisation or leaseback." £5m would be released immediately but £3m of that would go to repay Mike Ashley for previous loans. If the second £5m is drawn then that would be repayable within five years.

After supporter outrage, the security over the stadium was removed. Instead, security was handed over of the training ground, Edmiston House, Albion car park and club trademarks, including the badge. The loan had come from Ashley's Sports Direct and they would have the right to appoint two directors and had taken a further 26% in Rangers Retail giving them 75% of ownership and throttling the club's merchandise income. Rangers Retail would also receive a cut of shirt sponsorship income from 2017-18.

The Three Bears – Park, Letham and Taylor – had proposed an alternative £6.5m deal which mixed equity and debt. £4.5m of this would have been converted to shares and they would have matched the £10m available from Sports Direct. They were told by Derek Llambias that the offer would not be accepted if they did not promise to vote against EGM resolutions to remove certain board members.

Dave King had earlier requested an EGM to appoint himself, Paul Murray and John Gilligan to the board. The resolutions also called for the removal of Derek Llambias, Barry Leach, James Easdale and David Somers from the board. The board had six weeks to call the EGM.

The mockery and humiliation continued in the last days of the empire. Derek Llambias had stood up at the AGM and asserted that everything he would do "would be in the club's long-term interests". Proof of this masterplan was in the arrival, on the authorisation of Llambias, of five loanees from Newcastle United - Gael Bigirimana, Remie Streete, Haris Vuckic, Shane Ferguson and Kevin Mbabu.

The first that caretaker manager, Kenny McDowall, heard about it was on Sky Sports News. He also claimed he'd been told that the players, if fit, had to play. It later emerged that the players hadn't been given medicals before being signed. This made sense as two of the five (Birigimana and Mbabu) never featured at all whilst Streete lasted 44 minutes of a Scottish Cup tie against Raith Rovers. The cherry on the cake was that Newcastle United would be owed £500,000 if Rangers won promotion that season.

At a Newcastle fans forum, the board were asked what would happen if Newcastle United were to qualify for the Europa League. Their board responded that the club and "its owner would not put Newcastle United in a position where it would lose a European place because of Rangers." The Newcastle board also conceded that they were looking for clubs outside of England to act as feeder clubs for them and taking their talent on loan. It was a mouthwatering prospect for Rangers fans.

Kenny McDowall had taken over from Ally McCoist in December. McCoist had resigned and was placed on 'gardening leave' by the board as he had a 12-month notice period in his contract. His assistant,

Kenny McDowall, was appointed caretaker. He cut a reluctant figure. He was a coach that had been No. 3 under Walter Smith. He had no aspiration to manage the team and certainly not under the circumstances in which it was happening.

A month after taking over as caretaker, McDowall resigned on January 19. Like McCoist, he had a 12-month notice period in his contract. Unlike McCoist, he was not put on 'gardening leave'. The club now had two managers, both of whom had resigned with one of them sitting in the dugout every week, like a hostage. A credible, functioning board would have dealt with the situation in a way that would allow the club to salvage something from the season. That did not happen.

The board were now trolling the support in a way that even Craig Whyte might have gasped. The location of the EGM was announced. It would take place in London. The first time the club had ever held such a meeting outside Glasgow. It was to be held at the Millennium Gloucester Hotel in Harrington Gardens. The venue held 500 people and recent AGM's had attracted over 1,500.

Someone must have informed the Millennium Gloucester Hotel that they were potentially getting over 1,000 angry Bears turning up at their hotel and the venue cancelled fearing "significant disruption to guests and neighbours". Not to be thwarted, the board moved to another London hotel, the Grange

Tower Bridge hotel. It was tragic. The Grange Tower Bridge hotel also decided that hosting the football equivalent of the last day of the Ceausescu's was not something they wished to happen at their venue. And they cancelled. The board eventually conceded to hosting the EGM at Ibrox Stadium.

On February 25, James Easdale resigned. On the same day, the Rangers Supporters Trust purchased 450,000 shares from Beaufort Nominees, previously a proxy for Sandy Easdale. The RST now had shares and proxies of 4.4%. Rangers First, another supporter group, held 2.25%. The following week, David Somers resigned, packing his trunk and taking his people skills elsewhere.

In a final act of defiance, the board, now consisting entirely of Derek Llambias and Barry Leach, began drawing down the second £5m loan from Sports Direct.

The AGM lasted 13 minutes and saw 85% of the vote go in King's favour. It was a "landslide victory", he said. It was fifth time lucky for Paul Murray and he was jubilant. "In my view, from May 6, 2011, it has been all wrong here. The minute the club was sold to Craig Whyte it was the wrong decision. I have made mistakes, but hopefully people will recognise that I tried to do the right thing every time. I have certainly put Rangers' interests ahead of my own." It was a deal that should have gone ahead years earlier. If the King/Murray offer of April 2011 had been accepted, the club would have handled any impending storm much better than Whyte could ever manage. His business prowess couldn't even extend to running a football team for six months. If the First-Tier Tax Tribunal had delivered its verdict earlier. Yes, HMRC would have appealed (figures were still being disputed 10 years later) but the club could have had more time to prepare, to plan and to find alternative solutions. If the Murray Group and Lloyds had not accepted the first boat that went past. The entire episode had been an avoidable waste of time.

EIGHT

March 2015 – April 2017

On the field, the damage done in 2014-15 was too much to repair by the time the new regime took over. Settlements were reached with Kenny McDowall and Ally McCoist. The McCoist settlement took a little bit longer. McCoist appeared at the 2015 AGM as a shareholder and took his place in the audience. There was media talk that McCoist and McDowall thought they may be rehired by the new regime. There's no evidence that this was being thought of by either side of the relationship.

Ally McCoist is a Rangers legend and both McCoist and McDowall had been part of a very successful management team at Rangers that had reached the UEFA Cup Final. Ally McCoist managed Rangers in unprecedented circumstances. It's unfortunate for him, and us, that he never had the stability and resources one would normally expect at Rangers. It was considered best for both parties to try something else.

Stuart McCall was appointed manager until the end of the season and managed to navigate the team to the play-offs where they fell at the final hurdle. McCall later reflected that the team had fitness issues when he arrived in March and it was impossible to fix them in the final two months of the season. Regardless, Dave King was scathing of the performance shown against Hibs in the play-off semi-final despite the team being victorious over the tie. There would need to be a major improvement on the playing front.

It's safe to say that's easier said than done. Mark Warburton was appointed manager in June 2015 and, initially, recruited well. The core of a team featuring the likes of James Tavernier, Danny Wilson, Martyn Waghorn and Wes Foderingham was put together for less than £1.5m. Promotion back to the Premiership was won easily and the team even managed a never-to-be-repeated win over Celtic in the 2016 Scottish Cup semi-final.

Off the field, the club immediately banned Derek Llambias, Barry Leach and Sandy Easdale from Ibrox. In May, Llambias and Leach were sacked from their roles.

One of King's few mistakes was to underestimate Ashley. Initially, King seemed to start from a position that Ashley was a businessman who would be motivated by purely business instinct and seek a mutually beneficial business relationship. This did not turn out to be the case. It was perhaps the most challenging aspect of King's chairmanship.

The board had inherited the 'onerous contracts', that Graham Wallace had described, plus new ones signed by the outgoing board in what seemed to be a 'scorched earth' policy. In January 2015, just over a month before he jumped before he was pushed, David Somers had signed a 10-year-deal, on behalf of Rangers, with Sports Direct. This saw Sports Direct earn 93p for every £1 spent on club merchandise. It led to a supporter boycott of merchandise. The contract also had a staggering seven-year notice period. Even if King had ended the contract when he walked in the door, it would last until 2022.

The news worsened. As part of the deal, the club was receiving £1 rent from Sports Direct for the Megastore at Ibrox Stadium. The club tried suing Charles Green, Imran Ahmad, Brian Stockbridge and Derek Llambias for not acting in the club's interest in the negotiation of commercial deals. Green, Ahmad and Stockbridge argued that a competitor bid would have forced Ashley to bid higher for naming rights. A disingenuous argument. Ex-Sports Direct executive Derek Llambias had signed the club up to a Partnership Marketing Agreement in November 2014 which signed advertising space over to Sports Direct for £1. The case ended in March 2017 when the club withdrew the action.

£1 rent. £1 naming rights. £1 advertising. The club was being throttled of its income and the chance to build itself back up.

Ashley called for an EGM on June 12 to demand a vote on the repayment of the £5m loan made by Sports Direct in January. The Rangers board countered by proposing a vote on renegotiating the Sports Direct contracts. King promised to reveal more detail on them at the meeting. The day before the meeting, Ashley secured an injunction at the High Court in London banning the directors from disclosing any details in the contracts.

The meeting went ahead without the presence of Ashley or anyone from MASH Holdings even though they'd called the meeting. When the votes came in, Ashley's resolution for immediate repayment of the Sports Direct loan was rejected by 53.65% of shareholders. The counter resolution put forward by the board to renegotiate the Sports Direct contracts was approved by 62.5% of shareholders.

In June, Stewart Robertson was appointed managing director. Robertson had been at Motherwell and had left there in January. The club was looking to 'build bridges', they said, and Robertson fitted the bill. He was a safe pair of hands and had around 10 years of experience in Scottish football, including time on the SPL board. Many supporters disagreed with the idea of forming partnerships and networking with other clubs. They were not ready or willing to draw a line under the events of 2012.

There was also a feeling that the club needed a more aggressive figure as a chief executive. Rangers had never really employed such an individual. Murray had run the club himself during the 1990's and the appointment of Bain in 2005 was the first long-term CEO the club had ever had. Murray had tried a couple of candidates in the 1980's and 1990's but they never lasted as the real power always resided in Murray's office. Bain was happy to work under such conditions.

Robertson was a chartered accountant and his brief was clearly more of a management role rather than an executive taking a strategic view. He would do the role he was asked to do and do it well. Some supporters felt that they wanted connections and influence over the media and politics that chief executives at other clubs seemed to have. Those influences, however, can be overstated.

It is unarguable that 2012 had highlighted the club's political isolation. Even the local MSP, Nicola Sturgeon (SNP), could not be found to comment or speak up for the club. And she's normally very keen to offer a quote on any subject under the sun.

The club was on the horns of a dilemma. It needed to be a working part of Scottish football to ensure its own success and that the game was run for the benefit of all, and not just one or two clubs. The way to do this was to build its own power base and form allies and connections with other clubs. But this would also involve moving on from 2012 and that was unpalatable for some.

In October, King stated that Sports Direct had continued to take legal action against the club, tying the club in endless legal battles and draining it of money on legal fees. Sports Direct had deeper pockets and could play this game all day. King assured supporters of, in spite of the gagging order, "the level of robustness with which the Club's interest has been and will be protected." King observed that supporters felt that the retail side benefitted Sports Direct more than it benefitted Rangers.

An example of this incessant legal activity would become public when Ashley's lawyers attempted to jail Dave King for contempt of court. They claimed he had committed a breach of the confidentiality injunction in an interview with Sky Sports. Rangers responded by proposing a resolution at the AGM to remove the voting rights of any shareholder involved in the running of another club. Ashley responded to that by demanding a judicial review of the SFA's decision to pass Dave King as "fit and proper."

And on it went.

At the AGM in November, King announced that he, Douglas Park, George Letham, George Taylor, Paul Murray and John Bennett would repay the £5m loan to Sports Direct. This would free up the securities on the loan and reduce Sports Direct's stake in Rangers

Retail back down to 49%. It was suggested at the AGM that the first three years of the shirt deal with Sports Direct had produced a single payment of £300,000 for Rangers. Naturally, the board could not confirm this.

Having been defeated at two tax tribunals, HMRC were finally successful in their appeal in the tax case at the Court of Session in November 2015. BDO confirmed that they would appeal. The verdict was met with feverish excitement in some quarters. In reality, the club had moved on, accepting the SFA and SPL investigations into the matter. BDO were dealing with the case from the 'oldco' perspective.

At the High Court in London, Mr Justice Peter Smith dismissed Mike Ashley's attempt to jail King for contempt of court. King said it was a "humiliating defeat" for Ashley. The judge asked David Quest QC, for Sports Direct, "'Is your client interested in having a relationship with Mr King, or does he just want to grind him into the dust?' Dismissing the application, Mr Smith said the "proceedings from first to last were designed to intimidate rather than to seek proper sanctions for an alleged breach" Sports Direct dropped the claim and paid legal costs of £400,000.

In February, King announced that Rangers had given formal notice to end their relationship with Sports Direct. The seven-year notice period had been activated. Ashley abandoned his court action with the SFA over Dave King and would have to pay another £120,000 in legal costs to the SFA and Dave King.

The release of Rangers Retail accounts detailed the full extent of the problem. Strips and merchandise turnover to April 2015 was £4.2m. £2.7m of this was to be paid as dividends to Sports Direct and Rangers. Paying Rangers 25%, prior to the loan repayment, meant Rangers' payment was reduced to £650,000. On top of this, Sports Direct were claiming £620,00 for closing Rangers' stores. The club was making a grand total of £30,000. The auditors did not sign off on the accounts due to "insufficient evidence".

It wasn't all doom and gloom. Craig Whyte was declared bankrupt in October 2015. Perhaps it could go on his mantelpiece along with his director ban. Ticketus had been pursuing him for £20m since 2012. They had finally discovered that Whyte's 'personal and corporate guarantees' were worthless. Typically, Whyte failed to turn up for the hearing, with Matthew Collings QC, for Ticketus, saying there had been a "a degree of radio silence" from Whyte.

In 2015, Craig Whyte, Paul Clark, David Whitehouse, David Grier, Gary Withey, Charles Green and Imran Ahmad were all charged over the "alleged fraudulent acquisition" of Rangers. All of them, bar Whyte, had their charges subsequently dropped and only Whyte stood trial.

The memorable win over Celtic in the 2016 Scottish Cup gave Rangers their first Scottish Cup Final appearance in 7 years and the chance to clinch the trophy whilst in the lower leagues. It would get a monkey off the club's back. Whether through complacency or fatigue, the team never got going in the Final against Hibs. The season had started with a 6-2 thrashing of Hibs at Easter Road. There is no question that the team had the upper hand over them across the season. Promotion had been clinched over a month earlier whilst Hibs were still trying, and failing, to gain promotion up until the midweek before the Final. Perhaps the players were simply not switched on. However, a 2-1 lead with 10 minutes to go should have been negotiated without a problem. There was increasing criticism of Warburton's failure to develop a Plan B and that the team remained susceptible to set pieces. Two goals were conceded from corner kicks in the final 10 minutes which resulted in a very disappointing 3-2 defeat.

For the second season in a row, the Rangers players and support were confronted with a pitch invasion from opposing supporters. The 2015 play-off defeat at Fir Park had seen Lee McCulloch struck in the face by a Motherwell supporter and mounted police had to dispel hundreds of Motherwell supporters attempting to get to the 'away end' to goad the Rangers supporters who, to their credit, did not react. Motherwell were charged with 'unacceptable conduct' by the SPFL and placed on an 18-month probation.

The 2016 Final ended with Hibs supporters racing onto the pitch, attacking Rangers players and goading the Rangers support. In a statement that reflected all their class, Hibs dismissed the violence as "over-exuberance" from their supporters. Neither did anyone from Hibs bother to contact Rangers to apologise. The initial media response mainly condemned Hibs and their support. But this could never last. Within days, comments of the 'Rangers fans aren't blameless' either were prevalent. The Daily Record went one better and ran a ludicrous article that blamed Rangers fans for stopping the police getting into Hampden Park to break up the Hibs fans on the pitch. That's right. The Hibs fans rioting and attacking Rangers players was down to Rangers fans. It makes sense now that you see it written down.

A complaint was made to the Independent Press Standards Organisation (IPSO). The Daily Record admitted the entire article had been based on an email received from someone claiming to be a police officer. So, basically, anyone. They had not contacted Rangers or any supporters' groups to verify the information. They had contacted the General Secretary of the Police Federation, one Calum Steele, who said it was "disgraceful" although he also wasn't there. The complaint was upheld and the Committee found that the newspaper had taken "insufficient steps to take care over the accuracy of the article."

The SFA dropped all charges against Hibs and Rangers. It was notable that Rangers were included in the list of charges at all. It was Hibs fans that invaded the pitch. It was Rangers players that were attacked. It was only this curious Scottish football notion of 'fairness' which involves charging both sides when only one side is to blame. When Celtic fans attacked referee Hugh Dallas and Rangers players in 1999, it mutated into the 'Old Firm Shame Game' as if both sides were equally culpable. This rule does not apply when Rangers are solely to blame. In that instance, Rangers are solely to blame and should be punished.

Finding the right manager is the challenge for every football club. And it was certainly proving difficult. The 2016-17 season had perhaps seen an unrealistic level of optimism relative to the player recruitment and standard of the squad at the time. It was hit and miss. Celtic had been beaten in the Scottish Cup semi-final but over the course of a season that is much more difficult and requires different qualities.

The relationship between Warburton and King had deteriorated. The expensive signing of Joey Barton from the EPL had lasted a month before he and Warburton fell out. The club paid off the remainder of the contract. It had been a costly mistake.

Warburton ended up going to Nottingham Forest having stated he hadn't spoken to them. It was a badly handled episode all round.

The club then embarked on a risky strategy of appointing Pedro Caixinha, who had been managing in Qatar. He was said to have done well at interview. In some respects, it was understandable. The club had ongoing issues with revenue streams not being fully maximised. The damage to the club was such that it needed to accelerate growth some other way. One way was maybe to throw a 'double six' in appointing a manager. Every supporter and every club fantasises of finding the next Jose Mourinho or Alex Ferguson hidden away in some backwater. It very rarely happens.

NINE

April 2017 - May 2018

Craig Whyte stood trial at Glasgow Sheriff Court in April 2017 charged with fraud and a second charge of financial assistance under the Companies Act. Whyte was represented by Donald Findlay QC, who had been invited onto the board of Rangers in 1991 by David Murray. This golden era lasted until 1999 when some drunken shenanigans saw Findlay resign from the board. He later said he felt suicidal about the whole rum business. Now he would get the chance to grill Murray in the witness box and he would do so with some relish. BBC Scotland hailed the trial as perhaps "Findlay's finest hour". It was certainly something that would never be forgotten.

The trial didn't really tell us much we didn't already know. The Murray Group was in financial trouble in 2011. Lloyds were keen to sell pending the HMRC case and as part of a greater restructuring of Murray's financial position. Murray would be allowed to spin Murray Metals from the distressed group and purchase it for £1 if he agreed to the sale of Rangers and the repayment of the Lloyds debt. Both Lloyds and Murray were 'heavily incentivised' for the sale to happen. Murray had gambled the future of Rangers for the sake of owning Murray Metals.

The defence essentially hinged around the proposition 'had David Murray been, in his words, duped?' The conclusion was that he hadn't. Whyte's defence team sought to argue that the Murray Group and Lloyds didn't really care where the funds came from and, therefore, had not looked too closely. The Murray Group and Lloyds hadn't lost anything in the transaction either. It was Ticketus and the Rangers support that paid the price. Whyte had fraudulently obtained money from Ticketus and used it to fund his acquisition. He had fraudulently submitted proof of funds to the Murray Group and Lloyds. He had lied to the Rangers board and the Rangers support about the source of his funding but, Findlay argued, no financial loss had been sustained by the Murray Group or Rangers.

The charge of financial assistance, as described by Lord Tyre at Whyte's disqualification hearing, was defended by Findlay as being good for Rangers because it freed them from the debt they had with Lloyds. It was certainly one interpretation of events.

Craig Whyte did not give evidence in his defence. Alex Prentice QC, prosecuting, said Whyte had made "dishonest representations" that he had the money for the takeover. Whyte took "active steps" to conceal the source of funding from the Murray Group and Lloyds. On the second charge, Mr Prentice said "the money used to pay the bank debt was Ticketus money, which became the club's money. He then arranged a loan to Wavetower to pay the debt. That, ladies and gentlemen, amounts to financial assistance." It seemed straightforward. Mr Prentice called the case "relatively simple", which it was.

White collar criminal trials can fail because of their complexity and longevity. In the famous case of Robert Maxwell's sons, Kevin and Ian, they were acquitted in 1996 after a trial that lasted eight months. Many observers felt the trial had overwhelmed the jury and they'd simply lost track of what had happened and when. Whyte's trial only lasted six weeks and, on the face of it, was not particularly complex.

Findlay said Whyte was simply a "fall guy" and tried to bring in the previous board, the corporate governance of the club, Ally McCoist's contract, Walter Smith's transfer budget, anything to misdirect away from the key facts of the case. Whyte was not on trial over David Murray's running of Rangers. But it worked. The jury of seven men and five women found Whyte not guilty after two hours of deliberation.

In fairness to him, Whyte did not seem perturbed at any point by the trial. Perhaps he was used to it. He would happily pose outside the court during a lunch break for a selfie with a couple of Calton's fellow capitalist class.

Dave King had flown to Glasgow with the expectation that he would be called to give evidence but the Crown changed this at the last minute. None of the former directors would be called to give evidence. King expressed his disappointment at the "manner in which it was prosecuted". He felt Police Scotland had done a good job but "the Crown failed to prosecute it as well as it had been prepared for them."

Collectively, the whole business had been an embarrassment. The Scottish legal system had taken another hammering and public confidence in it was at an all-time low.

In June 2017, the club attempted to reset their relationship with Sports Direct with a new 12-month contract. King called it a "fresh start", an "end of the dispute with Sports Direct" and that the financial arrangements between both parties had been "transformed". As part of the deal, Mike Ashley sold his stake in Rangers to Club 1872 and investor Julian Wolhardt. Supporters called off their boycotts of official retail and merchandise in light of this new dawn.

Whether the club was badly advised or was simply outflanked, this new entente cordiale did not last. Rangers had paid Sports Direct £3m to replace the previous contract. But, as King noted, there were always "angles" with Sports Direct. One of those angles was that Sports Direct had the right to match any distribution deal. A new kit deal with Hummel, signed in April 2018, saw Sports Direct go to the High Court in London to block the sale of the kit to supporters.

Rangers had wanted to sign a new deal with a third party but Sports Direct had the contractual right to be given the opportunity to match any offer. Rangers were forced to settle out of court and pay the legal costs for Sports Direct. Supporters' groups immediately reinstated their boycott of Sports Direct. There seemed to be no end in sight. At the AGM, King described Sports Direct as "relentless" and said they were "determined to litigate." The inability to have a normal retail and merchandise operation was highly damaging. Effectively, the Megastore at Ibrox Stadium was unable to sell Rangers' own kit for two years.

It was not the only legal battle that took up King's time. Days after King and the Three Bears had bought their stakes in Rangers in January 2015, an "anonymous shareholder" had contacted the Panel of Takeover and Mergers to allege that King and the Three Bears had acted "in concert" and not independent of each other. King was deemed by the Panel to have been the "principal member" of the group and, therefore, the Panel obliged him to make an offer of 20p per share to all shareholders for the purchase of their shares.

The "anonymous shareholder" had been the then chairman, David Somers, acting in the "impartial" manner for which he was renowned.

King regarded the move as "pointless", arguing, not unreasonably, that the price would be not be attractive to many shareholders and that other shareholders, especially supporters, would be unwilling to sell in any case. Dave King is no pushover. There then followed a four-year legal battle where King was threatened with contempt of court. In March 2017, he was ordered by the Takeover Appeal Board to make an offer for the remaining 65% of shares which would cost him around £11m. He was ordered by another court in December 2017 to make the offer to which King replied that he was "penniless."

For the purposes of the offer, King's takeover group was said to hold 34% of the club. They would have to own 50% of the club at the end of the offer for it to be accepted. Eleven shareholders, including supporters' group Club 1872 and Ally McCoist, accounting for 38% of the shares, agreed that they would not accept the offer. A total of 13.07% of shareholders (including the Easdales) accepted the offer but this took the King group to 47.12%, short of the 50% threshold.

It had been, as King predicted, a waste of time but an expensive one at that. It had cost King around £600,000 to make the offer and cost Rangers around

£50,000 in financial and legal advice in relation to the offer. It was vexatious and pointless and perhaps that was the whole point. King's time, energy and money was taken up dealing with such matters and it had all served to act as a distraction and a drain on his and the club's resources.

Things weren't going much better on the field. Pedro Caixinha was delivering some unusual results, to say the least. The return to European football was ended in embarrassing fashion in a result that could almost be argued as grounds for instant dismissal in itself. League form was patchy and the team had lost to Motherwell at Hampden in the League Cup semi-final. Some key players in the dressing room had taken against him. There was a claim that the team was training as though in a high-temperature environment (like Qatar, for example) and thus lacking the intensity to which Rangers faced every week.

He was financially backed more than Warburton had been but to no obvious improvement in the team. A parting of the ways was inevitable and it came at the end of October. This allowed youth coach, Graeme Murty, to take over for the second time in less than a year.

Murty had taken the role on a caretaker basis in February and resumed that role. The plan by the board was to go for Derek McInnes of Aberdeen. A former Rangers player, he had also been talked up by the likes of Walter Smith as the ideal man for the job. The support was divided. Aberdeen weren't a particularly attractive side to watch and, despite Rangers' absence for four years, there were questions as to whether Aberdeen had really taken advantage of it. There was no great sadness that McInnes, for whatever reason, turned down the job. There was understandable bemusement.

What should the club do now? Unfortunately, not a lot. Graeme Murty carried on in his caretaker role until the end of the season. The last few weeks of the season were especially painful to watch. The club had now effectively wasted two seasons since coming back into the top flight, dithering around with poor managerial appointments and player recruitment.

TEN

May 2018 - Present

In May 2020, a 'clean slate' on retail and merchandise was announced by Rangers in a new deal with Castore Sports. Castore would supply kit and run the club's retail outlets including a renovation of the Megastore at Ibrox Stadium. Castore had no connection to Mike Ashley and it finally signaled the end of Ashley and Sports Direct's association with Rangers. A relatively new company, Castore encountered teething troubles and distribution issues with the kit. The scale of demand from the Rangers support seemed to catch them unawares. It was perhaps inevitable and a small price to pay for a more financially beneficial relationship from Rangers' point of view.

Craig Whyte released a book in February 2020. To promote his book, he was invited onto 'Off The Ball' a BBC Radio Scotland production that has been publicly flogged for nearly 30 years. It is hosted by Stuart Cosgrove and Tam Cowan, a comedy double act of two straight men. As they gently cupped and stroked Whyte, the pair tittered and giggled their way through Whyte's catastrophic running of Rangers that had left the club on its knees. It wasn't clear which of Whyte's many virtues – bankruptcy, misuse of company funds, disqualification, unpaid staff, unpaid creditors - most closely matched their values. A series of gentle and largely moronic questions were lobbed Whyte's way. When we needed Andrew Neil, we got Fran and Anna.

In November 2017, the UK Supreme Court had ruled in favour of HMRC in the tax case. This appeared to be the end of road. BDO then claimed HMRC had miscalculated the amount due. They had claimed for £94m but this was reduced by HMRC to £64m of which £48m related to EBT's. In total, £51m is currently disputed by BDO and they remain, as of December 2020, in negotiations with HMRC. Despite two tax tribunal defeats and a £30m miscalculation, Jim Harra, chief executive of HMRC, insisted they had "not made any mistakes."

A small group of Celtic fans had made the small tax case their life's work. This was the bill that Craig Whyte had promised to pay as part of his takeover. They called themselves the 'Requisition 12' boys after the requisition on their work which appeared in the Celtic AGM of 2013. There is a Rangers supporter on Twitter called Jas Boyd (@Jas72Boyd) who follows this very closely and has done good work on it. In essence, it seems this troop felt that Celtic were owed money, in some way, because the SFA should not have licenced Rangers to play in Europe in 2011-12 as the small tax bill was due.

Rangers had disclosed the tax bill to the SFA as of June 30, 2011 and they were permitted, within the rules, to have played in Europe in 2011-12. UEFA confirmed this was correct. The Requisition 12 boys changed the date to March 31, 2011. But the bill was not overdue at that point. UEFA agreed with this too. The bill had to be overdue from the previous period – December 31, 2010 – which it wasn't.

Rangers did not participate in European competition from 2012-13 to 2017-18, in any case. It's not clear what punishment the Requisition 12 boys wanted. If UEFA discovered an issue in 2011-12 with Rangers' participation in Europe then the punishment would have been for 2012-13 when Rangers did not play in Europe. The resolution narrowly lost by 97.18% at Celtic's 2020 AGM.

The administrators Paul Clark and David Whitehouse sued the Crown Office and Police Scotland for "unlawful arrest". They settled out of court in both cases in November 2020. Gerry Moynihan QC, representing the Lord Advocate, said the pair "should never have been prosecuted." David Grier and Charles Green are also suing the Crown Office and Police Scotland. Green is expected to receive a payout in 2021 with counsel for the Lord Advocate calling it a "malicious prosecution". Imran Ahmad is also suing the Crown Office.

Gary Withey passed away, aged 55, in October 2019.

The Lord Advocate, James Wolfe QC, is to make a public apology at Holyrood later this year. The Lord Advocate at the time the prosecutions were initiated was Frank Muholland QC, now judge Lord Mulholland. There are calls for a public inquiry into the Crown Office's handling of the case. Allegations of "malicious prosecution" are so serious and the costs of the case so high that such an inquiry would seem to be inevitable.

Murdoch MacLennan had been appointed SPFL chairman in July 2017. In 2018, Rangers had sought to have an independent investigation into his involvement with a company in Dublin called Independent News and Media (INM). INM had Celtic's Dermot Desmond and Denis O'Brien as significant shareholders. Rangers felt this was a potential conflict of interest. Rangers also queried MacLennan's inappropriate use of language when discussing Rangers. The SPFL refused to hold an investigation.

The appointment of MacLennan to the SPFL had even made the pages of Private Eye. The Eye had a long-standing animus with "Shifty" MacLennan, as they called him. The Eye wondered how MacLennan could perform his duties to the SPFL impartially given his hatred of Rangers. When managing director of the Daily Record in the 1990's, MacLennan had stated that, when it comes to Rangers, "ah cannae stand the bastards." He had refused to take an executive box at Ibrox but did have one at Parkhead and Hampden. He wanted the Daily Record to focus on negative coverage of Rangers. How could someone like that perform their duties in the SPFL in a fair manner? Following in the little shoes of people like Roger Mitchell, it would be a difficult task, surely.

Due to the worldwide COVID-19 pandemic, the 2019-20 Scottish football season was suspended on March 13, 2020. Rangers were sitting in 2nd place, 13 points behind the leaders but with a game in hand. They also had two matches against the leaders still to play. There was potential to cut the gap to 4 points with six other games to play.

From the outset, Rangers wanted the season to restart. UEFA wanted the season to restart. From very early on, however, the SPFL started a campaign of claiming that the only way to 'progress' was to end the season. In a grisly throwback to 2012, clubs were being threatened that they wouldn't get any prize money if they did not accept the SPFL's wishes. Rangers argued that money could be loaned from the SPFL to any clubs needing emergency funding and repaid from prize money when the season had restarted.

On April 11, the SPFL proposed a vote to end the leagues and decide promotion, relegation and prize money on a points-per-game basis. The proposition required 75% of clubs in each division to vote in favour of it. The resolution was expected to fail as

Partick Thistle (who would have been relegated, with a game in hand, under this proposal) and Inverness Caley Thistle had voted against it. They believed Dundee would also vote against it. Dundee said they had voted against it. But, by a magical coincidence, Dundee's email, the very email that would have ended the proposition, didn't arrive. It was sitting in the junk folder, they said. Don't you hate it when that happens? And then when Dundee did send it, it had changed. The vote had changed.

This was Scottish football in 2020. Emails go missing. Votes are altered. Trophies are awarded by email. Mics are muted at meetings so awkward questions can't be asked. Teams get relegated with a quarter of the season to go. And everyone smiles and does the conga.

Hearts were four points behind Hamilton with eight games to play. Relegation would have been unfair and financially damaging to them. Their chief executive, Ann Budge, was strung along with the prospect of league reconstruction that was never going to happen. She had been played. Budge had been patronised as a fine example of the new owner in Scottish football. When it came to the crunch, she discovered she had as much power in Scottish football as an asthmatic ant.

The leagues in England, Spain, Italy and Germany restarted, as did the Champions League and Europa League. Even the Scottish Cup was restarted with player eligibility rules ripped up. If the will was there, it seems, action would follow.

Rangers called for Neil Doncaster to be suspended and offered to fund an independent investigation into the voting scandal that had taken place. It required at least 32 of the 42 clubs to vote for it but, in the end, only 13 clubs – Rangers, Hearts, Aberdeen, Livingston, Partick Thistle, Stranraer, Falkirk, Inverness CT, Stenhousemuir all publicly supported it – thought transparency and good governance of the game was worth having. A third of the clubs had voted to investigate the SPFL. It was hardly a ringing endorsement for Neil Doncaster.

In some ways, 2020 was a continuation of 2012. Neil Doncaster, legal gofers, investigations, inquiries. Stewart Regan had gone and the SFA had plucked from obscurity someone called Ian Maxwell. During the pandemic and the voting scandal, Maxwell gave the impression of an actor appearing in the wrong movie. It was not clear he was operating independently. The roots of problems that were apparent in 2012 were still embedded in 2020. The club would need to continue to make its case for major reform of the game in Scotland for the long-term good of everyone.

Towards the end of 2020, Dave King announced he would sell his shareholding, over a three-year period, to supporters' group Club 1872. It would take Club 1872 from under 5% to a 25% stake in the club.

But it would also require Club 1872 raising its membership from a currently reported 8,000 members to 20,000 members to fund the £13m purchase. The news took Rangers and many supporters by surprise. Rangers received the news at short notice although King denied there had been any fall-out. It was, he said, an attempt to leave a legacy behind and ensure that the events of 2012 could never be repeated. With supporters owning a quarter of the club, it would be "Never Again" that the club could fall into the wrong hands.

Greater supporter involvement is a desirable goal and there have been various Rangers supporters' groups committed to that idea for the last 20 years. However, there is unquestionably an element of the Judean People's Front/The People's Front of Judea about the Rangers support. It is a broad church with a wide range of opinion and personalities. It can be challenging to find consensus in that environment. Club 1872 has its critics among the support and would certainly need an overhaul of its membership structure to ensure fair representation if it was to attain real power at the club.

If nothing else, at least the destination of King's shares is clear. And King had nothing left to prove. He would often say that no-one had ever put more money into Rangers than him. He had been convinced to part with £20m in 2000 by David Murray. He never saw that money again. He had committed millions since 2015 to restore Rangers back to the top of Scottish football. If he chose to sell his shares to supporters then that was up to him.

Rangers could never repay what Dave King, Douglas Park, George Letham, Paul Murray, John Bennet, and others, have done since 2015. The club wasn't heading for an appalling event like in 2012. It was just drifting out to sea, floating on apathy and fatigue, going nowhere. The club would have won promotion, eventually, and then competed for the odd cup and fought for a top four place in the top flight. A shadow of its former self. Rangers only have hope and a future now because of the boardroom changes in 2015, regardless of who takes the credit.

But getting it right off the field is only one part. Getting it right on the field is the other part. When the move for Steven Gerrard was announced in April 2018, it was met, in some quarters, with scepticism and some derision. Gerrard was both too inexperienced to manage Rangers, it was said, and also too big to manage Rangers. He was a Liverpool and England legend and one of the most famous names in world football. Why would he come to Scotland? And yet he did. Some 10,000 supporters gathered at Ibrox, in scenes not seen for a new signing for over 20 years, to welcome him to the club on May 4, 2018.

Gerrard brought a backroom team from Liverpool and set about trying to restore the standards for which the club had been known. He identified that the playing squad, and the support, had been 'scarred' by the previous decade. There had to be a stronger mindset, higher standards, a more professional environment than had been at the club for some time.

It was never going to be an overnight transformation. It would take time to learn new habits, build confidence and self-belief. Results improved domestically and in Europe, where the club was enjoying its best run of results in 20 years. Over three seasons, the team had negotiated 11 qualifying ties to reach the Europa League group stages three season in a row. They had twice progressed from the group stages.

There was no question of significant progress on and off the field. The only thing missing was a trophy. In one of the most one-sided cup finals in a long time, Rangers dominated Celtic in the 2019-20 League Cup Final but lost to a highly disputed goal. Two promising league campaigns had petered out in the second half of each season as the team seemed to struggle to maintain consistency.

Season 2020-21 was looking pivotal for Gerrard. Perhaps not quite make-or-break but a third season without a trophy would have been difficult to defend. Rangers had to hit the ground running and there was little room for error. Starting with a 1-0 win at Pittodrie on the opening day, the team went on a relentless run of form in the league. After beating Celtic for the third match in a row at the start of 2021, the team now sat 19 points clear at the top of the table albeit Celtic had 3 games in hand. The team was unbeaten in the league and enjoying its best start in 50 years. On and off the field, the club seemed in its best position for years. Ten years after Whyte and his chums staggered down Edmiston Drive, the club is on the verge of clinching the long-awaited 55th title. The journey is complete.

*

Printed in Great Britain
by Amazon

13995091R00088